WORDS THAT HURT,
WORDS THAT HEAL

WORDS THAT HURT, WORDS THAT HEAL

REVISED EDITION

*How the Words You Choose
Shape Your Destiny*

Rabbi Joseph Telushkin

wm

WILLIAM MORROW
An Imprint of HarperCollinsPublishers

HarperCollins books may be purchased for educational, business, or sales promotional use. For information, please email the Special Markets Department at SPsales@harpercollins.com.

Originally published in 1996 by William Morrow, an imprint of HarperCollins Publishers.

FIRST WILLIAM MORROW PAPERBACK PUBLISHED 1998.
FIRST WILLIAM MORROW REVISED EDITION PUBLISHED 2019.

Designed by Diahann Sturge

Library of Congress Cataloging-in-Publication Data has been applied for.

ISBN 978-0-06-289637-7

19 20 21 22 23 LSC 10 9 8 7 6 5 4 3 2 1

For Shlomo Telushkin
of blessed memory, and
Bernard "Bernie" Resnick
of blessed memory

My father and my uncle:
two men of golden tongues and golden hearts,
whose words healed all who knew them

An old Jewish teaching compares the tongue to an arrow. "Why not another weapon, a sword, for example?" one rabbi asks. "Because," he is told, "if a man unsheathes his sword to kill his friend, and his friend pleads with him and begs for mercy, the man may be mollified and return the sword to its scabbard. But an arrow, once it is shot, cannot be returned."

CONTENTS

WORDS THAT HURT,
WORDS THAT HEAL

PART ONE

THE POWER OF WORDS TO HURT

Introduction:
The Twenty-Four-Hour Test

IN RECENT YEARS, whenever I have lectured throughout the country on "Words That Hurt, Words That Heal: How the Words You Choose Shape Your Destiny," I've asked my listeners if they can go for twenty-four hours without saying any unkind words *about*, or *to*, anybody.

Invariably, a minority raise their hands signifying yes, some people laugh, and quite a large number call out, "No!"

"All of you who can't answer yes," I respond, "must recognize how serious a problem you have. Because if I asked you to go for twenty-four hours without drinking liquor, and you said, 'I can't do that,' I'd tell you, 'Then you must recognize that you're an alcoholic.' And if I asked you to go for twenty-four hours without smoking a cigarette, or drinking coffee, and you said, 'That's impossible,' that would mean that you're addicted to nicotine or caffeine. Similarly, if you can't go for twenty-four hours without saying unkind words about or to others, then you've lost control over your tongue."

At this point, I almost always encounter the same objection: "How can you compare the harm done by a bit of gossip or a few unpleasant words to the damage caused by alcohol and smoking or coffee?"

Is my point overstated? Think about your own life: unless you, or someone dear to you, have been the victim of terrible physical violence, chances are that the worst pains you have suffered in life have come from words used cruelly—from ego-destroying criticism, excessive anger, sarcasm, public and private humiliation, hurtful nicknames, betrayal of secrets, rumors, and malicious gossip.

Yet, wounded as many of us have been by unfairly spoken words, when you're with friends and the conversation turns to people not present, what aspects of their lives are you and your companions most likely to explore? Is it not their character flaws and the intimate details of their social lives—precisely those aspects of your own life that you would not like to hear others talking about?

If you don't participate in such talk, congratulations. But before you assert this as a definite fact, monitor yourself over the next twenty-four hours. Note on a piece of paper every time you say something negative about someone who is not present (without noting what was said—that would be too time-consuming). Also record when others do so too, as well as your reactions to their words when that happens. Do you try to silence the speaker, or do you ask for more details?

To ensure the test's accuracy, make no effort to change the contents of your conversations throughout the next day, and don't try to be kinder than usual in assessing others' character and actions. (Note your kind comments as well, but don't go out of your way to increase them during this test period.)

Most of us who take this test are unpleasantly surprised.

Our negative comments about those who are absent is but one way we wound with words; we also often cruelly hurt those *to whom* we are speaking.[1] For example, many of us, when enraged, grossly exaggerate the wrong done by the person who has provoked our ire. The anger we express that is disproportionate to the provocation (as often occurs when parents rage at children) is unfair, often inflicts great hurt and damage, and thus is unethical. How many of you have endured excessive outbursts of rage from another person? Similarly, many of us criticize others with harsh and offensive words or are unable to have a disagreement without provoking a quarrel. Some of us are prone to belittling or humiliating other people, even in public. Because the damage inflicted by public humiliation can be devastating (as noted later, it has even led to suicides), Jewish law questions whether anyone guilty of this offense can ever fully repent. Hurtful speech can, of course, be far less extreme. Have you ever muttered a sarcastic comment that made the person to whom you were speaking feel demeaned or foolish?

Many otherwise "good" people often use words irresponsibly and cruelly in part because they regard the injuries inflicted by words as intangible, and therefore they minimize the damage words can inflict. Thus, for generations, children taunted by playmates have been taught to respond, "Sticks and stones may break my bones, but words [or names] will never hurt me."[2] In our hearts, we all know that this saying is untrue. Even the child who chants "sticks and stones" knows that words and names do hurt him or her. The statement usually is an attempt at bravado by a child who more likely feels like crying.

The National Committee for the Prevention of Child Abuse has compiled a list of disparaging comments made by angry parents to children, including:

"You're pathetic. You can't do anything right."

"You disgust me. Just shut up!"

"Hey, stupid. Don't you know how to listen?"

"You're more trouble than you're worth."

"Get outta here. I'm sick of looking at your face."

"I wish you were never born."

Does anybody really believe that a child raised with such abuse truly thinks that "sticks and stones can break my bones, but words will never hurt me"?

The old Jewish teaching related in the epigraph to this book compares the tongue to an arrow. "Why not another weapon, a sword, for example?" one rabbi asks. "Because," he is told, "if a man unsheathes his sword to kill his friend, and his friend pleads with him and begs for mercy, the man may be mollified and return the sword to its scabbard. But an arrow, once it is shot, cannot be returned."[3]

The rabbi's comparison is more than a metaphor. Words can be used to inflict devastating, sometimes irrevocable, suffering. A penitent thief can return the money he has stolen, but one who damages another's reputation through malicious gossip (what is often labeled "character assassination") or who humiliates another publicly can never fully undo the damage.

As powerful as the capacity of words to hurt is their ability to heal. The anonymous author of a medieval Jewish text, *The Ways of the Righteous* (*Orchot Tzaddikim*), spends pages warning of the great evils routinely committed in speech. "With the tongue one can commit numerous great and mighty transgressions such as . . . talebearing, mockery, flattery and telling lies." But with words rightly used, he reminds his readers, "one can also perform limitless acts of virtue."

I remember reading a letter of gratitude sent by the nationally known preacher Reverend William Stidger (1885–1949) to an elementary school teacher who had given him great encouragement when he was her student decades earlier. A few days later, Stidger received a response, written in a shaky hand.

My dear Willie: I want you to know what your note meant to me. I am an old lady in my eighties, living alone in a small room, cooking my own meals, lonely, and seeming like the last leaf on a tree. You will be interested to know, Willie, that I taught school for fifty years and in all that time, yours is the first letter of appreciation I have ever received. It came on a cold blue morning and cheered my lonely old heart as nothing has cheered me in many years.[4]

Later, I relate a story from perhaps the best-known lawyer today in the United States, Alan Dershowitz, whose life—as an insecure teenager—was permanently transformed by *five* words spoken to him by a drama counselor at the summer camp where he was working (see pages 175–176). For Allen Sherman, the comic song writer of "Hello Muddah, Hello Faddah," it was *six* words spoken by his grandmother that healed a humiliation that had earlier caused him to slam a door and hide in his bedroom (see pages 185–186). And for Avi, a career criminal and drug addict estranged from his family, it was a verbal image created by the psychiatrist Dr. Abraham Twerski that started him on the road to becoming a law-abiding citizen devoted to extricating other drug addicts from lives of crime and purposelessness (see pages 206–208).

ANXIOUS AS I am for you to dive in and read this book, please take the twenty-four-hour diagnostic test first. Monitor how often you say needlessly critical, hurtful, and even cynical things *about* and *to* the people around you. Even if you are unhappy with the results, don't be discouraged. The way you speak is something you can change. And if you're willing to make the effort, you can start changing quickly. Today.

Perhaps the most surprising thing you will learn is the extent to which control over your tongue, accompanied by the practice of healing speech, will not only change for the better the lives of all those with whom you interact but change your own life as well. You might think I'm exaggerating, but I'm not. Healing words—both those we direct toward others and those directed toward us—create courage. Courage creates vision. With vision and courage, we become unafraid to take risks and are willing to hold on to our vision and work toward it. This, in the final analysis, is what shapes our destiny.

CHAPTER 1

The (Insufficiently Recognized) Power of Words to Hurt

The gossiper stands in Syria and kills in Rome.
—Jerusalem Talmud, *Peah* 1:1

IN A SMALL Eastern European town, a man went through the community slandering the rabbi. One day, feeling suddenly remorseful—and mindful of just how unfair many of his comments had been—he begged the rabbi for forgiveness and offered to undergo any penance to make amends. The rabbi told him to take a feather pillow from his home, cut it open, scatter the feathers to the wind, then return to see him. The man did as he was told, then came back to the rabbi and asked, "Am I now forgiven?"

"Almost," came the response. "You just have to do one more thing. Go and gather all the feathers."

"But that's impossible," the man protested. "The wind has already scattered them."

"Precisely," the rabbi answered. "And although you truly wish to correct the evil you have done, it is as impossible to repair the damage done by your words as it is to recover the feathers."

THIS FAMOUS TALE is a lesson about slander, of course, but it also is a testimony to the power of speech. Words said about us define our place in the world. Once that "place," our reputation, is defined—particularly if the definition is negative—it is very difficult to reverse.

It is perhaps for this reason that the Jewish tradition views words as tangible (in Hebrew, one of the terms for "words" is *devarim*, which also means "things") and extremely powerful. The Bible clearly acknowledges the potency of words, teaching that God created the world with words. As the third verse of Genesis records: "And God said, 'Let there be light,' and there was light."

Like God, human beings also create with words. We have all had the experience of reading a novel and being so moved by the fate of one of its characters that we felt love, hate, or anger. Sometimes we cried, even though the individual whose fate so moved us never existed. All that happened was that a writer took a blank piece of paper, or opened a blank screen, and through words alone created a human being real enough to evoke our deepest emotions.

That words are powerful may seem obvious, but the fact is that most of us, most of the time, use them lightly. We choose our clothes more carefully than we choose our words, though what we say *about* and *to* others can define them indelibly. That is why ethical speech—speaking fairly of others, honestly about ourselves, and carefully to everyone—is so important. If we keep the power of words in the foreground of our consciousness, we will handle them as carefully as we would a loaded gun.

Unfair speech does more than harm its victim: it also is self-destructive. The psychiatrist Antonio Wood notes that when we speak ill of someone, we alienate ourselves from that person. The more negative our comments, the more distant we feel from their object. Thus, the one who speaks unfairly of many people comes to distance and alienate himself from many individuals, and as

Dr. Wood notes, alienation is a major cause of depression, one of the most widespread disorders in America.

The avoidance of alienation is but one way in which we can benefit when we refrain from unethical speech. People who minimize the amount of gossip in which they engage generally find that their connections to others become more intimate and satisfying. For many, exchanging information and opinions about other people is an easy, if divisive, way of bonding with others. But those who refrain from gossiping are forced to focus more on themselves and the person to whom they are speaking. The relationship thereby established almost invariably is emotionally deeper.

In addition, when we make an effort to speak fairly to others and avoid angry explosions, we find that our social interactions become smoother. Admittedly, when you're angry at someone, maintaining a good relationship with that individual might seem irrelevant. But consider—particularly if you have a quick temper—whether you've ever heard yourself say, "I don't care if I never speak to him [or her] again!" about someone with whom you are now friendly. People who learn to speak fairly avoid going through life regretting the cruel words they said and the needless ending of friendships.

In the larger society, too, we are in urgent need of more civilized discourse. Throughout history, words used unfairly have promoted hatred and even murder. The medieval Crusaders didn't wake up one morning and begin randomly killing Jews. Rather, they and their ancestors had been conditioned for centuries to think of Jews as "Christ-killers" and thus as less than human (or worse, as allies of the Devil). Once this verbal characterization took hold, it became easy to kill Jews.[1]

African Americans were long branded with words that depicted them as subhuman ("apes," "jungle bunnies," "niggers"). The ones who first used such words did not choose these terms at random and for no reason. They hoped that such words would enable whites to view blacks as different and inferior to themselves. This was important because if whites perceived blacks as fully human, then supposedly "decent" people could never have arranged for them to be kidnapped from their native lands, beaten, branded, and enslaved.

Unfair, often cruel, speech continues to poison our society. I remember in the early 1990s a very popular and influential—perhaps the most influential—talk show host repeatedly labeled those feminists he regarded as radically pro-choice, and radical in other ways as well, "feminazis." Given that the Nazis—and the government they established—are regarded as about the most evil people in history, the word "Nazi" should be removed from our vocabulary except when speaking about the Nazis themselves, or people who truly model themselves on them. To call a feminist like Gloria Steinem a "feminazi," as this talk show host did, is rhetoric that, in my view, is unethical, makes rational discourse impossible, and unintentionally mocks the sufferings of the Nazis' real victims.[2] Unfortunately, over the following decades this host has continued to find the term "feminazi" useful in dismissing some of those whom he opposes.

This sort of verbal incivility has characterized some highly partisan liberals no less than conservatives. When George H. W. Bush was elected president in 1988, a prominent congressman who soon went on to become House majority leader, along with a major city mayor who had earlier served as the ambassador to the United Nations, commented that not since the days of Hitler and Goebbels had a political campaign been built so deliberately on the technique of the Big Lie.[3] What an irony! In the very act of condemning Bush's campaign for its supposed lies, these men told a vicious and much bigger untruth.

With similarly overwrought and unethical language, one of the country's most influential senators reacted to one of President Ronald Reagan's Supreme Court nominations by asserting: "Robert

Bork's America is a land in which women would be forced into back alley abortions, blacks would sit at segregated lunch counters, rogue police could break down citizens' doors in midnight raids, school children could not be taught about evolution, [and] writers and artists could be censored at the whim of government."[4] Those familiar with Judge Bork's views and judicial record knew that the statement was an amalgamation of untruths and misleading half-truths. But the senator's agenda was neither accuracy nor fairness; it was defeating Bork's nomination.

IT IS IMPORTANT to emphasize that all of us—not just political candidates—can be passionate about our convictions without denigrating the intelligence and morality of those with whom we disagree. Unfortunately, this is hard for many people to do. Every four years during presidential campaigns, I ask audiences at lectures if they can think of a *single* reason someone might vote for the candidate whom they oppose that doesn't reflect badly on either the voter's head or heart. I rarely find liberals or conservatives who can do so.

This is very unfortunate, because it means that passionate liberals and passionate conservatives often presume that about half of the population is deficient in either intelligence or character.

Yet people don't have to think about political disagreements in this way. Robert Dole, the Republican presidential candidate in 1996 and a man by no means averse to fighting vigorously on behalf of what he believed, nonetheless took care to remind his followers that "the Democrats are our opponents, not our enemies." In 2008, when Republican presidential candidate John McCain found himself at a rally in which people were denouncing his opponent, Barack Obama, as a "liar" and a "terrorist," McCain shook his head, took the mike, and said, "He's a decent family man, a citizen that I just happen to have disagreements with on fundamental issues, and that's what this campaign is all about." McCain in no way felt the need to minimize or downplay his political opposition to Obama, but he didn't feel—as do many people on both sides of the political divide today in America—that he had to denigrate his opponent as a human being: "If I didn't think I'd be one heck of a better president, I wouldn't be running," McCain declared. But he then went on: "[Having said that], I will respect him. I want everyone to be respectful. Because that's the way politics should be conducted in America."

Or at least that's the way political *campaigns* should be conducted in America, or anywhere—with a focus on issues and the candidates' disputes about those issues. But political campaigns—and political dialogue in general—increasingly focus not on issues but on personalizing conflict and dehumanizing one's opponents. And unfortunately, once people feel contempt, dislike, and hatred for the candidate they oppose, it is quite easy for those feelings to spill over into contempt and hatred toward those who voted for that candidate. Why wouldn't it? If all you know about a person is that he supported the candidacy of a person you believe to be a vile human being, then why, so the thinking goes, should you have any respect, let alone affection, for such a person?

In consequence, the level of discourse over these past years, by both the right and the left, has continued to deteriorate—reaching a low point in the 2016 presidential campaign. To the extent possible in discussing actual events, I prefer not to name names (though, for a variety of reasons, this is not always feasible). In the events I am discussing, candidates, instead of critiquing the policies of their opponents, attacked their very personhood. Thus, the aforementioned John McCain, who was captured and endured torture (often several times a week) and abuse as a prisoner of the North Vietnamese during the Vietnam War, has long been regarded as a hero by almost all Americans, both liberals and conservatives, but not by the

Republican candidate who eventually won the nomination: "He's not a war hero," Donald Trump said of McCain. "He was a war hero because he was captured. I like people who weren't captured." This was a particularly mean-spirited comment about a man who had fought for the United States and endured torture and imprisonment in horrifying conditions for five and a half years. (McCain also refused to accept an offer of early release because the North Vietnamese would not release other American prisoners who had been captured before him.)

Other comments made by the candidate displayed a disturbing lack of fairness and civility. Thus, while there is a long and sad history of men mocking the looks of women they regard as unattractive or whom they simply dislike, this sort of cruel banter did not normally become part of a presidential campaign—until this candidate made it so. One of his opponents in the primary race to secure the Republican nomination was a highly distinguished businesswoman and the former CEO of a major company. (I am omitting her name because, while she is deservedly famous, I suspect that the incident I am about to recall is not an aspect of her life she wants to be associated with.) How did her opponent evaluate her as a candidate? "Look at that face. Would anyone vote for that? Can you imagine that as the face of our next president?"

When this woman launched her campaign, I assume she had prepared herself to have some of her political positions severely challenged and attacked. But I doubt she had prepared herself to have her physical looks mocked. No candidate, man or woman, should have to expect that.

I suspect that some—I hope not many—of Trump's supporters found such a comment amusing, but it was cruel. Who would not be offended and hurt to be publicly described as particularly unattractive? Similarly, Trump had every right to criticize the political views of another woman, a major media figure, but what made his remarks about this woman so memorable was one particular observation that she "is unattractive both inside and out. I fully understand why her former husband left her for a man. He made a good choice." Obviously, it was this comment—about what had to have been a very painful event in this woman's life—that most stuck in listeners' minds.

A person can speak like that—publicly ridiculing the sad and painful events in another person's life—only if he has ceased to relate to the other person as if they were like himself, a person with feelings.

The response of some passionate liberals to conservatives have likewise often been cruelly unfair and uncivil. How else can one assess Congressman William Clay's 1980s claim that President Ronald Reagan was "trying to replace the Bill of Rights with fascist precepts lifted verbatim from *Mein Kampf*?" (I am identifying Congressman Clay by name because his statement was so extreme and untethered to reality that people might think I made it up.)

For a congressman to make such a remark would seem unthinkable. But the congressman did say that. And what is one to make of a statement by a prominent South Carolina congressman concerning the direction of the United States under President Donald Trump: "Having studied history and having taught history, I can only equate one period of time with what we are experiencing now, and that was what was going on in Germany around 1934 right after the 1932 election when Adolph Hitler was elected chancellor."[*]

When the congressman was challenged about his implied comparison of Trump to Hitler, he walked back his comment a bit, saying that it would be more accurate to compare President Trump

---

[*] *Editor's note*: Hitler was elected in January 1933.

to Mussolini—in other words, to compare him to the most famous fascist who ever lived rather than to the most famous Nazi.

What should seem self-evident and is most important about these types of comments is that they are untrue. If Ronald Reagan preferred *Mein Kampf* to the Bill of Rights, then the congressman making this accusation would not have been serving in the House of Representatives but would have been in jail, or worse. (In actuality, President Reagan completed his second term in 1989, while Congressman Clay remained in office until 2001.)

Civil discourse in America becomes increasingly difficult when a liberal congressman compares Republican attacks on the health care overhaul pushed by President Obama to the Nazi propaganda of Joseph Goebbels (the Nazi minister of propaganda). The congressman soon had to issue a clarification: "I want to be clear that I never called Republicans Nazis. Instead the reference I made was to the greatest propaganda master of all time." But obviously, invoking Goebbels's name in the midst of a political fight that had nothing to do with World War II or the Holocaust can only engender ill will and prompt people to associate their political opponents with Nazis and Nazi-like propaganda.[5]

There are consequences to the dehumanizing of one's opponents. To cite one example—and there is no shortage of others—in October 2017, a mass shooting occurred in Las Vegas directed against country-music concertgoers. Fifty-eight people were murdered and 861 were wounded. The reaction of the vice president and senior legal counsel at CBS—obviously a substantial, even coveted, position—was: "I'm actually not even sympathetic because country-music fans often are Republican gun-toters." Hence, by this lawyer's logic, there is no reason to regret that fifty-eight people died—each one of them someone's mother, father, or child—and because they are Republicans, and maybe even conservative Republicans, the country is better off without them. (I am omitting the woman's name on the assumption that she actually might be ashamed of having made such a heartless statement.) CBS, realizing that its very moral credibility was at stake, fired this executive.

When I use the word "dehumanize," I mean it quite literally. Some of the comments I have cited here—not all—are cruel specifically because the persons making them have ceased to see the person or people whom they dislike as fellow human beings.

In certain segments of popular culture, such dehumanization has been going on for several decades. A musical genre, "gangsta rap," pioneered in the 1980s, contains lyrics that glorify killing police and raping women. The album *The Geto Boys*, by the group of the same name, includes this horrendous couplet:

I dug between the chair and whipped out the machete
She screamed, I sliced her up until her guts were like spaghetti.

Another lyric in the same album speaks of the need to "stab the girl" in her breasts and "just cut her to bits."[6]

Marian Wright Edelman, the African American founder and president of the Children's Defense Fund, expressed her horror at the cruelty of such lyrics and their massive disrespect to women. Having herself been raised in a culture in which men were encouraged to "woo the hearts of women" by opening doors for them and giving up their seats when only one seat was available, Wright Edelman was enraged by "the filthy, disrespectful, and misogynistic lyrics of Snoop Doggy Dogg and Dr. Dre and others who shamelessly dishonor our foremothers, grandmothers, mothers, sisters, and daughters by referring to them as 'hos' [slang for 'whores'] and 'bitches.' The shame of those who buy this debasing music is matched or exceeded only by those who profit so greatly from it— the record companies and the performers."[7]

Gangsta rap is only one manifestation of contemporary music's incendiary usage of language. When Axl Rose, lead singer of Guns N' Roses (famous for the lyric "I'll rip your heart in two and leave you lying on the bed"), attended a "homecoming" concert in Indianapolis some years ago, he told his cheering fans that "kids in Indiana today are just like prisoners in Auschwitz."[8] The talk show host Michael Medved commented: "When Rose later defended these appalling remarks in conversations with reporters, no one thought to ask him the obvious question: If he really believes that parents are like guards at a Nazi death camp, wouldn't teenagers be perfectly justified in killing them in order to achieve their freedom?"[9]

The use of language to humiliate, degrade, and enrage likewise typifies many of the lyrics of Eminem. To cite just one example (and there are many others), a song entitled "Kill You" contains the following rhyme: "Slut, you think I won't choke no whore, / Till the vocal chords don't work in her throat no more."[10]

I cite Eminem because he is by no means a minor figure. His songs and their accompanying videos routinely garner 50 million or more viewers within days of release.

A nineteenth-century story tells of a man who saw a large sign over a store, PANTS PRESSED HERE. He brought in his pants to be pressed, only to be told, "We don't press pants here, we only make signs."

The "sign makers" of our time are those who compare their political opponents or parents to Nazis and who glorify the mutilation of women—in short, those who use words to incite rather than inform.

Violence, however, is only one possible result of unethical speech. Another is the destruction of what decent people consider their most important possession, a good name. Raymond Donovan, secretary of labor in President Reagan's administration, was the victim of a long campaign of rumors and innuendo that finally culminated in a criminal prosecution. After running up legal bills in excess of $1 million, he was acquitted of all charges. When he emerged from the courtroom and reporters swarmed around him for his comment, Donovan posed a bitter question: "Where do I go to get my reputation back?"

Truly—as the anguished Ray Donovan knew—once feathers have been scattered to the wind, they can never be fully recovered.

PART TWO

HOW WE SPEAK ABOUT OTHERS

CHAPTER 2

The Irrevocable Damage
Inflicted by Gossip

Lashon hara, the whispering campaign that cannot be stopped, rumors it's impossible to quash, besmirchment from which you will never be cleansed, slanderous stories to belittle your professional qualifications, derisive reports of your business deceptions and your perverse aberrations, outraged polemics denouncing your moral failings, misdeeds, and faulty character traits—your shallowness, your vulgarity, your cowardice, your avarice, your indecency, your falseness, your selfishness, your treachery. Derogatory information. Defamatory statements. Insulting witticisms. Disparaging anecdotes. Idle mockery. Bitchy chatter. Malicious absurdities. Galling wisecracks. Fantastic lies. *Lashon hara* of such spectacular dimensions that it is guaranteed not only to bring on fear, distress, spiritual isolation, and financial loss but to significantly shorten a life. They will make a shambles of the position that you worked nearly sixty years to achieve. No area of your life will go uncontaminated. And if you think this is an exaggeration you really are deficient in a sense of reality.

—Philip Roth, *Operation Shylock*

A gossip always seeks out the faults of people; he is like the flies who always rest on a person's dirty spot. If a person has boils, the flies will ignore the rest of the body and sit on the boil. And thus it is with the gossip. He overlooks all the good in a person and speaks only of the evil.

—*The Ways of the Righteous* (*Orchot Tzaddikim*)

WHAT DOES A good guest say? 'How much trouble has my host gone to for me. How much meat he set before me. How much wine he brought me. How many cakes he served me. And all this trouble he has gone to for my sake!' But what does a bad guest say? 'What kind of effort did the host make for me? I have eaten only one slice of bread. I have eaten only one piece of meat and I have drunk only one cup of wine! Whatever trouble the host went to was done only for the sake of his wife and children.'"[1]

These two takes on the same party, reported in the Talmud nearly 2,000 years ago, gets straight to the heart of ethical speech: the fact that, given a willing ear, many of us, if not most, are bad guests and often disloyal friends. It is infinitely more interesting to look for others' flaws than to praise their good qualities. How much more satisfying it is to chew over the fact that so-and-so is having an affair, was fired from his job for incompetence, has filed for bankruptcy, or, less seriously, tells very unfunny jokes and then laughs at them uproariously than it is to discuss how good a husband, how loyal an employee, how financially circumspect, and how wonderful a raconteur he may be.

How strange that dinner parties, where we have partaken of a host's hospitality, so often seem to prompt critical "postmortems." My hunch is that more speculative, and often unkind, gossip and character analysis are exchanged immediately after people leave a dinner party than at any other time. How often during the ride home from a dinner party have you speculated about your host's wealth, marriage relationship, aesthetic sensibilities, taste in food, intelligence, or children's personalities?

It is obvious how very unfair such talk is. I know that when my wife and I invite people over for dinner or a party, we work incredibly hard for many hours, sometimes even several days, to make the evening as pleasant as possible for our guests. It hurts to think that they might share critical observations about us as they drive home afterward. I don't think I am being paranoid in fearing that this is what many of them do because, regretfully, I know how often I have done so myself.

When leaving the home of someone who has worked hard to provide you with a pleasant evening, the simplest and fairest rule to follow is to say nothing disparaging about them. If you find that you are incapable of abiding by this rule, at least don't speak negatively during the ride home. Hold off for a day; perhaps when you finally make your comments, they will be toned down. Before saying anything, think about the effort this person expended to make the gathering pleasant, and ask yourself if it is appropriate to respond with critical observations.

Few things seem more unjust than partaking of other people's hospitality, thanking them, and then, like a spy, utilizing information you acquired in their home to cut them down. If you think that your comments about others are rarely malicious, then ask yourself: Would you be willing to make the same remarks directly to your host? If the answer is no, then why make these remarks to others? (On the subject of gossip with one's spouse or significant other, see pages 55–56.)

The impulse to be a "bad guest" violates the following biblical injunction: "You shall not go about as a talebearer among your people" (Leviticus 19:16). This directive is the foundation of the

Bible's guidelines on ethical speech—and it appears only two verses before the Bible's most famous law: "Love your neighbor as yourself" (Leviticus 19:18).

Because the biblical commandment is so terse, it is difficult to know exactly what is meant by "talebearing." Does it mean that you are forbidden to talk about any aspect of other people's lives, such as telling a friend, "I was at a party at so-and-so's house last night, and it's absolutely amazing what they've done with their kitchen"? Or does the verse outlaw only damning insinuations ("When Sam went away on that business trip last month, I saw his wife, Sally, at a fancy restaurant with this very good-looking guy, and she didn't see me because they were too busy the whole time making eyes at each other")? Is it talebearing to pass on true stories ("Betty told me that Sally confessed to her that she's planning to divorce Sam")?

The Bible itself never fully answers questions of this nature. But starting with the early centuries of the Common Era, Jewish teachers elaborated upon the biblical law and formulated, in ascending order of seriousness, three types of speech that people should decrease or eliminate:

1. Information and comments about others that are non-defamatory and true.

2. True but negative stories (in Hebrew, *lashon ha-ra*): Such information lowers people's esteem for the person about whom it is told. A subdivision is tattling (in Hebrew, *rechilut*)—telling Judy, for example, the critical things that Ben said about her.

3. Lies (in Hebrew, *motzi shem ra*): statements that are negative and false. Rumors commonly fall into this category, as often they are both negative and false.

NONDEFAMATORY AND TRUE REMARKS

The comment "I was at a party at so-and-so's house last night, and it's absolutely amazing what they've done with their kitchen" is nondefamatory and true. What possible reason could there be for discouraging people from exchanging such innocuous, even complimentary, information?

For one thing, the listener might not find the information so innocuous. While one person is describing how wonderful the party was, the other might well wonder, *Why wasn't I invited? I had them over to my house just a month ago*, or, *Funny that they had the money to redo their kitchen since they pleaded poverty when I asked them to contribute to the new hospice.*

The more important reason for discouraging "innocuous" gossip is that it rarely remains so. Suppose I suggest that you and a friend spend twenty minutes talking about a mutual acquaintance. How likely is it that you will devote the entire time to exchanging stories about the person's niceness?

Maybe you will—that is, if the person about whom you're speaking is Mother Teresa. Otherwise, even if the person being spoken about is a very good person, the conversation will often take on a negative tone. This is because, for most of us, exchanging critical evaluations of others is more interesting and enjoyable than exchanging accolades. If I say to you "Janet is a wonderful person, but there's just *one thing* I can't stand about her," on what aspects of Janet's personality do you think the rest of our conversation is likely to focus?

Even if you don't let the discussion shift in a negative direction, becoming an ethical speaker forces you to anticipate the inadvertent harm that your words might cause. For example, although praising a friend might seem like a laudable act, doing so in the presence of someone who dislikes her will probably do your friend's reputation more harm than good. Your words may well provoke her antagonist to voice her reasons for disliking your friend, particularly if you leave soon after making your positive remarks.

Strangely enough, the Bible depicts God as causing terrible damage to a righteous man by praising him in his enemy's presence. As the book of Job opens, God is surrounded by angels, and one of them is Satan, who informs God that he has been roaming the earth. The Lord asks Satan, "Have you noticed my servant Job? There is no one like him on earth, a blameless and upright man who fears God and shuns evil."

Satan accuses God of being naive: "Does not Job have good reason to be God-fearing? Why, it is You who has put a fence around him and his household and all that he has. You have blessed his efforts so that his possessions spread out in the land. But lay Your hand upon all that he has and he will surely blaspheme You to Your face" (Job 1:9–11).

Confident that Job will remain loyal to Him no matter what the provocation, the Lord permits Satan to do anything to Job except take his life. In short order, Satan arranges to have Job's ten children killed, his possessions destroyed, and Job himself afflicted with terrible maladies. Although the book of Job records a series of happy events at its ending, would anyone dispute that Job's life would have proceeded far more smoothly had God not chosen to praise him before Satan?

The danger of praise leading to damage is at the root of the book of Proverbs' rather enigmatic observation: "He who blesses his neighbor in a loud voice in the morning, it will later be thought a curse" (27:14).

Bible commentaries understand this to mean that if a person comes to public notice, even as a result of a neighbor's "blessing" (a positive association), the intense scrutiny engendered by his newfound fame ultimately will probably damage his good name—or worse.

Such was the fate that befell Oliver Sipple, an ex-Marine who saved the life of President Gerald Ford. While Ford was visiting San Francisco in 1975, Sipple saw Sara Jane Moore, who was standing next to him, aim a gun directly at the president. Sipple grabbed Moore's arm and deflected her aim so that the bullet missed the president. Overnight he became a national hero.

When reporters came to interview Sipple, he had only one request: "Don't publish anything about me." Unfortunately, his plea piqued the journalists' curiosity; within days, the *San Francisco Chronicle* and the *Los Angeles Times*, quickly followed by dozens of other newspapers, trumpeted the news that Sipple was active in gay causes in the San Francisco area.*

Of course, there is still prejudice against gays in the United States today, but there was far greater antagonism toward gays at that time. When a reporter confronted Sipple's mother in Detroit and asked her what she knew about her son's apparent homosexuality, she was visibly stunned, since she had known nothing about it. Of course, that was the reason Sipple had begged reporters not to write about his life. Shortly thereafter, his mother stopped speaking to him. When she died four years later, his father informed Sipple that he wouldn't be welcome at her funeral.

Devastated by the rupture in his relationship with his family, Sipple began to drink heavily and became increasingly withdrawn from those around him. A few years later, he was found in his apartment, dead at age forty-seven.

The *Los Angeles Times* reporter who publicized Sipple's homosexuality made this postmortem comment: "If I had to do it over again, I wouldn't."[2]

---

* Sipple was also outed by a prominent member of the gay community who thought it would be beneficial for the image of gays to make it known that the hero who saved the president was gay. This might well have been true, but it should have been Sipple's right to decide what information about himself he wanted to make known.

But why did he and the other reporters have to tell the story about Sipple in the first place? Sipple had saved the life of the president, and the entire country was deeply in his debt. Yet the insatiable curiosity of the press (and readers) to learn the "true story" about this new American hero caused them to search for a fresh angle. After all, how many times could they describe how he had caused Moore's gun to misfire? His action, while very heroic, became somewhat boring after two or three tellings.[3]

The Sipple case demonstrates the inadvertent damage that can be done even when people start out talking positively about others. *Unless we remain acutely conscious of the direction in which a conversation is heading, such talk is unlikely to remain innocuous* (especially from the perspective of the person being discussed).

NEGATIVE, MEAN-SPIRITED TRUTHS (*LASHON HA-RA*)

As a rule, most people seem to think that there is nothing morally wrong with spreading negative information about others as long as the information is true. Jewish law takes a very different view. Perhaps that is why the Hebrew term *lashon ha-ra* (literally "bad language" or "bad tongue") has no precise equivalent in English. For unlike slander, which is universally condemned as immoral because it is false, or gossip, which might or might not be true, *lashon ha-ra* is by definition true. It is the dissemination of *accurate* information that will lower a person's status. I translate it as "negative truths," or, as my friend the late Rabbi Israel Stein used to render it, "mean-spirited truths."

The *fairness* of negative information is particularly important but frequently overlooked by people who disseminate it. I often ask lecture audiences: "How many of you can think of at least one episode in your life that would cause you great embarrassment were it to become known to everyone else here?"

Usually, almost every hand goes up, except for those who have poor memories, who have led exceptionally boring lives, or who are lying. I suspect that most people who raise their hands are not concealing a history of armed robbery. Nevertheless, were a particularly embarrassing episode to become known to the public, it might disproportionately influence others' impressions of them. Because such information would probably be unusual, it might even become other people's primary association with the person, which of course is the very reason he or she wants it kept private. Thus, although such information is true, disseminating it would be unfair.

That is why Jewish law forbids spreading negative truths about anyone unless the person to whom you are speaking needs the information. (For examples of when and to whom such information should be revealed, see chapter 4.) Two centuries ago, Jonathan K. Lavater, a Swiss theologian and poet, offered a still-apt guideline that highlights the unfairness of spreading such information: "Never tell evil of a man if you do not know it for a certainty, and if you know it for a certainty, then ask yourself, 'Why should I tell it?'"

Intention also has a great deal to do with the circumstances in which it is prohibited to speak negative truths. A statement, depending on the context, can constitute a compliment, gossip of the nondefamatory sort, or the more serious offense of *lashon ha-ra*. For example, if you say that a person known to have limited funds gave $100 to a certain charity, this information would probably raise his stature because people will be impressed with his generosity. But if you say that a very wealthy individual gave $100 to the same cause, others' respect for him will be diminished, as this information makes him look miserly. Such a statement therefore is *lashon ha-ra*: it might be true, but it lowers respect for the person, and it is very unlikely that the person to whom you are relating this information really needs it.

Unfortunately, people are often undeterred from speaking negative truths. Such gossip is often so interesting that it impels many of us to violate the Golden Rule ("Do unto others as you would have others do unto you"). Although we would probably want similarly embarrassing information about ourselves to be kept quiet, many of us refuse to be equally discreet when it comes to others' sensitive secrets.

As noted earlier, the Golden Rule can be violated in another way as well. If you entered a room unnoticed and heard people talking about you, what would you least like to hear them speaking about? Most likely, your character flaws and/or the intimate details of your social life. Yet when you gossip with friends about others, what are you—if you are like most people—most likely to talk about? Is it not the character flaws and intimate details of the social lives of others?

The Jewish ethical injunction against unfair speech applies not only to the use of words but also to lowering another's reputation nonverbally. Making a face when someone's name is mentioned, rolling your eyes, winking, or saying sarcastically, "Yeah, he's a real genius, isn't he?" are all violations of the law. When I was growing up, a child would often say something positive about another, then clear his throat in such a manner as to convey that he really meant precisely the opposite. Since *lashon ha-ra* is regarded as anything that lowers another person's status, it is irrelevant whether the technique used to commit it is verbal or nonverbal. Jewish law designates this behavior as *avak lashon ha-ra* (the "dust of *lashon ha-ra*").[4]

Other examples of such behavior include innuendo ("Don't mention Paula's name to me. I don't want to say what I know about her"). It is equally wrong to imply that there is something derogatory about a person's earlier life ("Who among us who knew

Jonathan years ago would have guessed that he would achieve the success he has now?").

Such behavior encompasses a whole range of stratagems by which people sometimes damage reputations without saying anything specifically critical. For example, it is morally wrong to show someone a letter you have received that contains spelling mistakes if all you wish to do is cause the reader to have a diminished respect for the letter writer's intelligence. It is similarly wrong to show a person an unflattering photograph of another and for the two of you to laugh about the picture.

When it comes to *lashon ha-ra*, if your goal is to lower another person's status, then it can be done equally effectively through words, a sarcastic laugh, or sharing a letter that holds its writer up to ridicule. Each of these methods is effective, cruel, and wrong.

WHEN GOSSIP IS FALSELY ATTRIBUTED TO YOU

If a rumor circulates that you said something unkind about someone and it isn't true, you must make this known both to the person involved and to others. If you don't, the person slandered will remain justifiably hurt and angry. Compare the ways in which two different public figures dealt with this situation.

In *Attlee*, a biography of Clement Attlee, a British prime minister and longtime political adversary of Winston Churchill, the author, Kenneth Harris, notes the following incident:

> *After the war, one quip which went the rounds of Westminster was attributed to Churchill himself. "An empty taxi arrived at 10 Downing Street, and when the door was opened, Attlee got out." When . . . [a friend] repeated this, and its attribution, to Churchill he obviously did not like it. His face*

*set hard, and "after an awful pause" he said: "Mr. Attlee is
an honorable and gallant gentleman, and a faithful colleague
who served his country well at the time of her greatest need.
I should be obliged if you would make it clear whenever an
occasion arises that I would never make such a remark about
him, and that I strongly disapprove of anybody who does."*[5]

Compare Churchill's disavowal of this cruel, if witty, comment
with the behavior of a prominent former congresswoman toward
New York's onetime mayor Ed Koch. Unlike Attlee and Churchill,
the congresswoman and Koch had long been political allies; in fact,
he had campaigned for her when she ran for the U.S. Congress, as
she did for him when he ran for City Hall.

Several years later, this woman took a trip with New York City
mayor David Dinkins to lobby the Democratic Party to hold its
1992 national convention in New York City. In a newspaper article about the trip, she was quoted as saying that she was happy to
be traveling with Dinkins, whereas she would hate the thought of
spending a week with Koch. The latter, unaware of any falling-out
between them, was both incensed and confused.

A few months later, Koch was even more stunned when the
woman, launching a run for the U.S. Senate, called him at his law
office to solicit his support. In his memoirs, *Citizen Koch*, he records
the ensuing conversation:

*"Well . . . ," I said, "it's strange that you should call me, be-
cause you are the last person I would support."*

*"Why do you say that, Ed?" she said. "I thought we were
friends."*

*"I thought so too," I replied. I then reminded her of her
remarks from several months back.*

"Did I say that?" she said.

"Yes," I said.

"Well, I don't remember ever saying that."

"I have the clipping here at my office," I explained. "I can send you a copy to refresh your memory."

"Well, if I did say it," she allowed, "it must have been taken out of context."

"Did you write a letter to the editor, stating you had been quoted out of context?"

"No."

"Did you call the reporter, or send him a note, seeking a retraction?"

"No."

"Did you call me, to apologize, or offer an explanation?"

"No."

"Then it wasn't out of context," I said.[6]

Koch was right. If you have publicly said something cruel that you regret, call the victim of your remarks immediately and apologize. You can be sure that the person will have heard about it, and if you don't apologize, he or she has a right to assume that you meant precisely what you said.

In a column by the Pulitzer Prize–winning writer Bret Stephens, "When the White House Lies About You," he details a damaging and mean-spirited untruth told about him by a high-level White House official.[7] (The official tweeted that Stephens had publicly named a covert CIA officer.) What particularly provoked Stephens's anger was that, though the untruth might well have started as a mistake, the government official refused to correct it even after Stephens repeatedly informed him that the slanderous comment was untrue. To summarize Stephens's argument, and to play off Koch's comment as well, when you make a mistake and refuse to correct it, it ceases to be a mistake. It becomes intentional.

People simply don't forget cruel words directed against them or against someone they love. Should you be accused of having uttered such words, your only hope for making peace is to *deny* those words forcefully (and immediately), both privately and publicly, if they are untrue, and to *apologize* in the same manner if they are true.

TATTLING (*RECHILUT*)

A subdivision of *lashon ha-ra*, *rechilut*, is tattling—telling people the negative comments that others have made about them.

Several years ago, when a friend of mine announced her engagement, her sister repeated a remark made by their beloved uncle: "Mary's a very sweet girl, but Robert is much more accomplished and worldly than she is. I'm afraid that he's going to get bored with her."

For Mary, whose father had died when she was very young, her uncle's critical words were devastating. When she got married, she refused to walk down the aisle with him, as they had long planned. Today, several years later, their once warm relationship is almost nonexistent.

Coincidentally, I saw Mary's sister a short time later and asked her about this incident. The statement just slipped out, she told me; she had been chatting with Mary, and it suddenly occurred to her that she should know what their uncle really thought.

The sister's answer, a standard justification offered by people who transmit hurtful comments, seems inarguable in theory: Aren't we entitled to know whether the people who act warmly in our presence say cutting things when we are absent? In practice, however, the one small piece of "truth" transmitted by a gossip often makes a very false impression. Once Mary heard her uncle's comment, she concluded that it constituted his exclusive opinion of her. After all,

Mary's sister hadn't made a habit of repeating every complimentary observation their uncle had made about her.

While the uncle's comment may well have been unkind, in truth almost all of us have said hurtful things about people we otherwise love dearly. How many of us would be comfortable with our parents, children, spouses, and friends hearing every remark that we've ever made about them? "I lay it down as a fact," the great seventeenth-century French philosopher Blaise Pascal wrote, "that if all men knew what others say of them, there would not be four friends in the world." And as Mark Twain once said, "It takes your enemy and your friend, working together, to hurt you to the heart; the one to slander you and the other to get the news to you."

Of course, there are times when it is appropriate to pass on such information. If you hear someone saying that another person is dishonest and you know this to be false, you should both publicly dispute the statement and warn the person of what is being said about him. However, such extremely damaging statements are the exception. Generally, unless there is a specific, constructive reason to pass on negative comments, you should not do so.

While Jewish ethics generally forbid lying, you are permitted to be less than fully truthful when asked: "What did so-and-so say about me?" If the reply is likely to inspire ill will, you are permitted to fend off the question with a half-truth, omitting the negative comments the original speaker made. The Talmud itself cites even God as shading truth in this way. When three angels visit the ninety-nine-year-old patriarch Abraham and predict that within a year his eighty-nine-year-old wife Sarah will give birth, the Bible records that Sarah, who is listening nearby, "laughed to herself, saying, 'Now that I am withered, am I to have enjoyment, with my husband so old?'" In the next verse, God says to Abraham, "Why did Sarah laugh, saying, 'Shall I in truth bear a child, old as I am?'" (Genesis 18:12–13). God omits Sarah's reference to Abraham being too old to impregnate her, apparently fearing that Abraham will become incensed at his wife. From this incident, the Rabbis conclude that when human feelings are at stake, it is permissible to relate less than the whole truth ("to deviate from the truth," in the words of the Talmud), even if doing so conveys a false impression.

RUMORS

The *Washington Post* reporter Bob Woodward, along with Carl Bernstein, authored one of the great journalistic coups of the past century: the story of the Watergate cover-up. In the decades since, Woodward has been regarded as the most prominent investigative journalist in the United States. One would therefore expect such a professional to be acutely aware of the importance of *always* carefully checking sources for legal, not to mention ethical, reasons. But during the media uproar some years ago that greeted Senator John Tower's nomination as secretary of defense, Woodward, operating under a severe deadline for the *Post*, reported a retired air force sergeant's claim that he had witnessed Tower when he was publicly drunk and fondling two women at an army base.[8] According to Woodward's article, the man had witnessed Tower touching one woman's breasts and patting the other's buttocks. The article went on to quote the sergeant as saying that if one of his daughters had been the victim of such lewd conduct, he would have been "sent to Leavenworth"—the implication being that he would have assaulted Tower and been willing to go to prison as a result.

The air force sergeant was the only named witness in the article; Woodward referred to other "informed sources" who allegedly also were aware of the event, but he never specified who they were. Unsurprisingly, his article led many readers to conclude that Senator Tower was both morally and emotionally unfit to be a cabinet member.

Within a day of his article being published, it became known that Woodward's "eyewitness" had earlier been dismissed from the air force because of "mixed personality disorders with antisocial, hysterical features." In other words, Woodward's source was a severely disturbed individual who, it appears, had made up the story.

Confronted with this evidence, Woodward responded: "You report what you can get." He added: "And I wish I had [had] more time on that story to check."[9] But ethics dictate that you *don't* report what you can get; you only report stories that you have *overwhelming* reason to believe are true. (To the *Washington Post*'s credit, as Professor Larry Sabato has noted, the paper subsequently published a correction with a comparable front-page placement.)[10]

The Talmud teaches: "If something is as clear as the fact that your sister is forbidden to you as a sexual mate, [only] then say it."[11] In other words, before bandying about words that can destroy another person's reputation, be as careful as if you were holding a loaded gun.

This should be obvious, but many people deem it morally acceptable to report rumors, even though, from the perspective of the person damaged by a false story, the effect can be devastating. (I do not want to suggest that Woodward normally did so—he didn't.) This is particularly unfortunate, since so many rumors are both negative and, not infrequently, false. After all, when was the last time you heard something like, "Hey, did you hear that so-and-so is really a wonderful person?"

Casually spreading rumors is yet another violation of the Golden Rule. When we are the subject of an unpleasant rumor, we desperately do whatever we can to quash it. Yet when someone else is the rumor's subject, many of us spread it, oblivious to the pain we are causing its victim, and not even knowing for a fact whether it is true.

Ask most people whether they ever spread malicious lies about others, and they'll respond, "No," certain that they would never do such a thing. But if you spread a negative rumor that turns out to be untrue, that is exactly what you have done. Believing that your words might have been true affords little consolation to the person whose reputation you have damaged. Few people, after all, who get drunk and then drive do so with the intention of injuring or killing someone. But if you drink and drive, there is a good chance that you will eventually kill or hurt someone. If you pass on nasty rumors about others, sooner or later (and likely sooner) some of these rumors will turn out to be false and you will be guilty of spreading a malicious—possibly reputation-destroying—lie about someone.

Some years ago, I was conducting an ethics advice column for beliefnet.com and a woman forwarded to me an email she had received, claiming that the clothing manufacturer Tommy Hilfiger had been a guest on Oprah Winfrey's television program and that Oprah asked him if he had said the following: "If I had known that African Americans, Hispanics and Asians would buy my clothes, I would not have made them so nice. . . . I wish those people would not buy my clothes; they were made for upper-class whites." According to the email, Hilfiger had answered yes, whereupon Oprah asked him to leave the show. The email then urged all readers to give Hilfiger what he wanted and not buy any of his products.

The woman who forwarded me the email, a good friend, then added as a postscript: "As a person devoted to influencing people to act more morally, I thought you'd want to post this email and encourage others to act like my friend and me and start boycotting Tommy Hilfiger."

Of course, it turned out that Hilfiger had never said such a thing. Even before I checked into the rumor, I was quite certain it was untrue, for I was unable to imagine that a businessman like Hilfiger, even if he were a bigot, would say things on television that would cause large numbers of people to boycott his business. Businessmen want to increase the number of people who buy their products, not alienate them.

I wrote back to my friend, suggesting that she verify the rumor, as I had done. She did so, and quickly learned that it was a malicious falsehood. Hilfiger and his company, which featured models of all ethnic backgrounds in its advertising, were horrified that this rumor was circulating on the internet. Tommy Hilfiger was no bigot, and he hated being thought of as one.

I therefore suggested that, as a first step, she contact everyone to whom she had sent the email she sent me and tell them that she had made an error. I also suggested to her, as I do to all people who hear nasty rumors about someone, that she check out any subsequent rumors she hears very carefully before passing them on.

As is so often the case in life, we should apply the Golden Rule. If somebody heard such a rumor about you, how carefully would you want that person to check it out before sharing it? And if he passed it on without checking it out, and it was also untrue, how impressed would you be by his defense that he thought it was true?

As a general rule and unless there is an ethically compelling reason to pass on a rumor (see the following section), the best response to a rumor is to follow the advice of the apocryphal book of Ecclesiasticus: "Have you heard something? Let it die with you. Be strong; it will not burst you" (19:10).

Is this advice easy to follow? No. We all like to be thought of as being "in the know" and having access to information that others have not yet heard. But if the information you spread is nobody's business, that is morally wrong. And if it's both untrue and negative, that's worse than wrong. It might well be unforgiveable— certainly so if you don't try to undo the damage.

When You Can't Confirm the Truth of a Rumor
but Feel Ethically Obligated to Share It

In some instances, it is morally permissible to pass on a rumor privately—for example, when a physician is rumored to be practicing treatments that are harmful to patients, or a financial adviser is rumored to have lost a great deal of his clients' money. It is still forbidden, however, to present as definite something you don't know to be a fact. When you disclose "facts" that are only hearsay, the damage you inflict may be devastating and irrevocable. Therefore, even where another's safety or well-being mandates that you report a rumor, you must make clear that it is a rumor and requires further investigation. You should say, "I don't know this to be definitely true, but I've heard that so-and-so has made some very risky investments for his clients, and lost considerable amounts of money. I think you should check further into the matter before you invest money with him."

I know that just saying that can be very damaging to the object of the rumor, but saying nothing could be very damaging to the potential investor. I suppose the expression "being caught between a rock and a hard place" applies to situations like these. That is why, until I feel confident in my facts, I would speak only to people who might be interacting with the person in question, and I would emphasize that I don't know the rumor about that person to be factually true.

SLANDER

The most grievous violation of ethical speech is the spreading of malicious falsehoods, what Jewish law calls *motzi shem ra*, "giving another a bad name." Consider the following story, which appeared in *USA Today*:

A 9-year-old girl falsely accused a substitute teacher of sexual abuse and bribed 10 other kids to do the same, police said Tuesday.

The teacher [whose name I'm omitting, although it appeared in the article], 43, was cleared when police uncovered the plot.

[The man], who had been a substitute for about four weeks apparently had difficulty with the class his first day at Fuller Elementary School and sent some students to the office.

The child offered nine girls and a boy $1 each to report that [the teacher] fondled them.

The Cook County State's Attorney got the complaint May 9; investigators interviewed 14 children the next day "and by the end of the day we knew . . . that every allegation was false," says spokesman Andy Knot.

[The teacher] calls the incident "a nightmare. A lot of people were willing to crucify me."[12]

An especially troubling aspect of this story is that none of the ten children to whom the child offered a bribe seems to have refused it or to have reported her. They all seemed oblivious to the damage they would do to their victim. Yet to destroy somebody's good name is to commit a kind of murder. (In English, as noted, the same idea is conveyed through the expression "character assassination.")[13]

But of course it is not only children who pass on cruel, even vile, stories intended to hurt others; there is no shortage of adults who do so as well, though unlike the children in the *USA Today* story, they don't generally claim that they were the personal victims. And the ability to cause great damage to others has only been magnified in today's age of the internet. You can spread a damaging untruth on the internet and reach tens of thousands, even millions, of people in a matter of minutes. Even when you spread a rumor among fewer people, your victims can suffer enormous emotional damage. Such was the case with John Seigenthaler Sr., a lifelong journalist and free speech and civil rights activist. Seigenthaler had served in the early 1960s in Attorney General Robert Kennedy's office and was sufficiently close to Kennedy that he was one of the pallbearers at his funeral. Most people, as Daniel Solove notes in his book *The Future of Reputation: Gossip, Rumor, and Privacy on the Internet*, would be flattered to have an entry about themselves in Wikipedia, but Seigenthaler was shocked to find that his Wikipedia bio contained the following unmitigated lie: "John Seigenthaler Sr. was the assistant to Attorney General Robert Kennedy in the early 1960's [*sic*]. For a brief time, he was thought to have been directly involved in the Kennedy assassinations of both John, and his brother, Bobby. Nothing was ever proven."

Seigenthaler wrote about the horror of his experience in *USA Today*, a horror that was magnified when he learned that the same "scurrilous text" was found in Reference.com and Answers.com.

When Seigenthaler learned that Bell South Internet was the service provider for the person who had written this Wikipedia entry, he contacted the company to request assistance in correcting the matter. Bell South informed him that it knew the person's name but would not reveal it unless ordered to do so by a court. Getting a court order would, of course, involve an expensive lawsuit, and Seigenthaler, though very upset, didn't pursue the matter. (I have consistently found Wikipedia to generally be very reliable and have used it often in my research, but it is also true that the authors of its articles are unknown and very difficult for the average reader to trace.)

More than four months after the article had been posted, Wikipedia finally removed the defamatory accusation, and another person, outraged by the horrible injustice to Seigenthaler, was finally able to trace the IP address of the writer. It turned out that the man had posted the article as a prank to rile a coworker, and he apologized to Seigenthaler.

Seigenthaler, himself familiar from childhood with the story that opens this book—about the repentant slanderer who was told to cut up a feather pillow, scatter the feathers to the winds, and then retrieve them—commented bitterly, "That's how it is when you spread mean things about people." Slander can never be fully undone. There might well be some people who to this day think that Seigenthaler was somehow implicated in the Kennedy assassinations.[14]

In the age of the internet and its accompanying anonymity, the potential to be *motzi shem ra* and disseminate lies about people is greater than it has ever been.

Spreading lies about both individuals and groups of people has a long and horrible history. The most famous biblical example of mass slander with potentially genocidal results is provided in the book of Esther. Haman, adviser to the Persian king Ahasuerus, maliciously lies by telling the king that the Jews refuse to obey his laws. Like many liars, Haman is persuasive, and Ahasuerus soon empowers him to murder every Jew living in Persia and its 127 provinces (Esther 3:9–15).

Fortunately, Haman's lies are disproved and his murderous campaign thwarted. Too often, however, the victims of slanderous tongues are not saved. In the fourteenth century, during Europe's devastating Black Plague, antisemites and others seeking scapegoats spread the claim that Jews had caused the plague by poisoning Europe's wells. Within a few months, enraged mobs had murdered thousands of Jews. In the nineteenth and twentieth centuries, similar sorts of rumor-mongering bigots provoked the lynching murders of many African Americans in the South.

Literature is very familiar with the theme of individuals who spread malicious lies. Thus, in Shakespeare's thirty-eight plays, there is no villain more vile than *Othello*'s Iago, whose evil is perpetrated almost exclusively through words.

At the play's beginning, Iago vows to destroy the Moorish general Othello for bypassing him for promotion. Knowing Othello's jealous nature, Iago convinces him that his new wife, Desdemona, is having an affair with another man. The charge seems preposterous, but Iago repeats the accusation again and again and arranges the circumstantial evidence necessary to destroy Desdemona's credibility. Soon Othello comes to believe Iago. In the end he murders his beloved, only to learn almost immediately that Iago's words were false. For Othello, "Hell," as has long been noted, "is truth seen too late."

A similarly destructive tongue is possessed by Mary Tilford, the twelve-year-old protagonist of Lillian Hellman's classic play *The Children's Hour*. A precocious but vicious child, Mary is disciplined by one of her school's headmistresses. Fearful that some of her other misdeeds will soon be uncovered, she confides a scandalous "truth" to Mrs. Tilford, her grandmother: the school's two headmistresses are lesbian lovers. Within hours, the grandmother has alerted everyone to this "fact," and alarmed parents withdraw their children from the school.

Weeks later, the rumor is finally proven false, but by then the school has been shut down, one headmistress has committed suicide, and the other has broken off her engagement, certain that her fiancé does not fully believe that the rumor is untrue.

The grandmother feels deep remorse over what has happened. A normally moral person, she knows that she made insufficient efforts to establish the story's veracity before destroying the lives of two women. At the play's end, she appears at the surviving headmistress's house, willing to do anything to make amends. Of course, there is nothing she can do other than express some ineffective words of contrition.[15]

"Nobody ever gossips about other people's secret virtues," the British philosopher Bertrand Russell once noted. What is most interesting to many of us about other people are their character flaws and private scandals. Therefore, before you spread information or views that will lower the regard in which another is held, ask yourself three questions:

Is it true?

Even if true, is it fair?

Is it necessary?[16]

CHAPTER 3

The Lure of Gossip

In the future, all the world's animals will come together and confront the snake. They will say to him: "The lion stalks and then eats its prey, the wolf rips apart another animal and eats it. But you, what is the pleasure you derive in poisoning and killing a human being?" The snake will answer: "And what is the pleasure human beings derive in spreading malicious gossip [which humiliates and sometimes destroys others]?"

—Babylonian Talmud, *Ta'anit* 8a

AS A RULE, the rationale for wrongful acts is self-interest: embezzlers wish to make quick money, guilty defendants manufacture alibis to avoid being punished, and thieves break into a house because they desire another's possessions. But what do gossips gain by hurting other people's reputations?

Some 1,500 years after the Talmud set down the parable that opens this chapter, William Shakespeare conveyed a similar bewilderment about slanderers' intentions and actions:[1]

Who steals my purse steals trash, [. . .]
But he that filches from me my good name

Robs me of that which not enriches him
And makes me poor indeed. (*Othello* III, iii, lines 161–165)

Shakespeare's assertion seems inarguable. A person deprived of his good name by a slanderer is surely impoverished, while the slanderer seems to have gained no benefit. Or has he?

In truth, the benefits derived from spreading malicious gossip may be intangible, but they are no less real.[2] *The most important reason we gossip is to raise our status through lowering the status of others.* There's a tremendous psychological gratification in seeing someone else's social status decline.

Few of us are willing to acknowledge that our motivation in gossiping is so self-serving. Rather, we would have others believe (and perhaps believe ourselves) that we are talebearers only because the intimate details of other people's lives are inherently so interesting. If that is so, why, then, do we almost always restrict gossip to our social equals or superiors? People rarely talk about the intimate details of the lives of their cleaning woman or gardener. The only gossip that makes us feel better about ourselves is precisely that which lowers the public esteem of those with whom we are in "status competition," our social peers or superiors.

I remember first having this thought some twenty-five years ago, while witnessing the extraordinary public fascination with the unhappy marriage of England's Prince Charles and Princess Diana; at one point in 1992, three of the fifteen books on the *New York Times* best-seller list were detailed accounts of Charles and Diana's clearly unhappy marriage. At one level, this fascination reflected a certain cruel pleasure in seeing members of the British royal family "brought down a peg." Beneath the "tsk-tsks" was gratification in learning that a royal heir apparent and his beautiful wife apparently were leading painful and unhappy lives.[3] Learning endless details about "the misery of the rich and famous" seems to make many people feel better about their own lives.

Many of us also derive great enjoyment from seeing a comedown for those who summon us to a morally upright life. Thus, a clergyman caught or rumored to have been involved in a scandal, particularly a sexual one, finds himself the subject of particularly nasty and unrelenting gossip. Such talebearing relieves a strong moral pressure on us, for if the individual making moral demands of us can be shown not to abide by such demands him- or herself, their downfall seems to free us from moral responsibility.

In their pathbreaking *Harvard Law Review* article on "The Right to Privacy," Samuel Warren and future Supreme Court justice Louis Brandeis noted the enticing element in nasty gossip: it appeals "to that weak side of human nature which is never wholly cast down by the misfortunes and frailties of our neighbors."[4] The word "weak" could as easily have been replaced by "malicious." We might well have other, more elevated personality traits, but our motives for exchanging tidbits about other people's miseries are rarely noble.

Another way we seek to elevate ourselves is by retailing inside information about others so that we'll be perceived as being "in the know." As Dr. Samuel Johnson observed two centuries ago, "The vanity of being trusted with a secret is generally one of the chief motives to disclose it."

Does Dr. Johnson's dictum seem overstated? If you think so, then consider the following, admittedly unlikely, scenario: The president of the United States chooses you as his confidant. He speaks with you regularly, sometimes several times a day, shares his innermost thoughts, bounces ideas off you, and otherwise solicits your advice. The only condition attached to your relationship is that you are forbidden to tell anyone, *ever*, about it. The president also will never mention to anyone, either during his time in office or afterward, that he knows you or has ever spoken to you.

For most of us, I suspect, the satisfaction and pleasure of having such access to the president would largely evaporate if we could tell no one about it, neither now nor in the future. A primary motive for gossiping is that, in bragging to others about our acquaintance with important people and important things, we're implying that *we* must also be important.

This motive for gossip is already apparent in children and adolescents. In *You Just Don't Understand: Women and Men in Conversation*, Deborah Tannen cites the conclusion of anthropological and sociological research that teenage girls are more likely to betray friends' secrets than boys. Why? Among adolescent boys, Tannen explains, status tends to be based on athletic accomplishments or, perhaps more important, on the ability to prevail in a physical or verbal fight. Among girls, status is linked more to being connected to the "in crowd": "Girls get status by being friends with high-status girls: the cheerleaders, the pretty ones, the ones who are popular with boys. If being friends with those of high status is a way to get status for yourself, how are you to prove to others that a popular girl is your friend? One way is to show that you know her secrets, because it is in the context of friendship that secrets are revealed."[5]

Thus, a girl who is insecure about her attractiveness or popularity proves that she rates high status through the very action that indicates that she is an unworthy friend.

The issue, of course, goes far beyond teenagers and the betrayal of secrets. It seems to be universally accepted that we will be regarded as important people if we know interesting gossip with which others are unfamiliar. In his book *Chutzpah*, Alan Dershowitz tells a story that reveals a fairly typical kind of gossipmonger:

> *My mother is vacationing at a Jewish hotel in the Catskill Mountains, and is sitting around with a group of older women. One of them hears my mother's name and, without*

realizing that she is my mother, launches into a discussion of that other Dershowitz, the Harvard professor. "Such a wonderful boy he is, but why did he have to go off and marry that [non-Jewish woman]? All the smart and successful ones do it, Henry Kissinger, Ted Koppel . . . ? Why?"

My mother, playing dumb, strings along the know-it-all: "How do you know that Dershowitz married a non-Jew?"

Mrs. Know-it-all knows: "My son's cousin is his best friend. He was at the church where they had the wedding."

My mother responds: "Well, I heard that he married a Jewish woman."

"So you heard wrong," Mrs. K.I.A. assures my mother. "That's the story his family is putting out, can you blame them?"

At this point, my mother can't hold back. "Alan Dershowitz is my son. I was at the shul [synagogue] where he married Carolyn Cohen, whose father's name is Mordechai and whose mother speaks fluent Yiddish. So what do you say about that?"

"Oh, I'm so glad it wasn't true!" Mrs. K.I.A. says in obvious relief, but quickly adding, "How about Henry Kissinger, is his wife Jewish too?"[6]

Silly as this case sounds (can you imagine inventing a story that a cousin of yours attended a church wedding that never happened?), it illustrates what Jack Levin and Arnold Arluke, sociology professors at Boston's Northeastern University, accidentally discovered in a study of gossip: that "inventiveness" (untruthfulness) is all too common. For their experiment, Levin and Arluke, seeking to see how quickly gossip spread among students, had hundreds of flyers printed announcing a wedding ceremony to be performed in front of the Northeastern student union building. The flyer read: "You are cordially invited to attend the wedding of Robert Goldberg and

Mary Ann O'Brien on June 6 at 3:30 in the afternoon." They circulated the flyers throughout the campus, tacking them on bulletin boards, stacking them in classrooms, and so on. Robert Goldberg and Mary Ann O'Brien were fictitious figures, and Levin and Arluke distributed the flyers on June 7, the day after the wedding supposedly occurred.

A week later, when they polled students to learn how many had "heard" about the wedding, they discovered that 52 percent had. "More amazingly," they note, "12 percent told us they had actually attended [it]! These students said they were there on June 6; many of them described the 'white wedding gown' worn by the bride and the 'black limo' that drove the newlyweds to their honeymoon destination."[7]

The students' responses seemed so bizarre that the two sociologists checked to see if a campus wedding might have occurred on or about the same time, but none had. In their quest to be perceived as people who had the "inside scoop about the big event," 12 percent of the students polled were willing to tell a flat-out lie. The desire to seem important can impel otherwise rational people to act in a pathetically dishonest way.

How ultimately meaningless such artificial elevation of one's status is. How much more satisfying it is when others raise their opinion of us because of our accomplishments.

A third reason we often speak ill of others—and this might be the most important one—is to exact revenge against people who have wronged us but whom we are too timid to confront. This timidity is at the core of much gossip. It might well be natural to have this impulse, for if we complain to the offending party, we risk being hurt again by his or her response. We can easily find consolation, as well as justification for our anger, when others share our feelings about the offense and the offender.

This form of gossip usually is particularly unfair. Because we want others to share our anger, we often fail to describe very precisely the offense committed against us. If we did, our complaints might not strike other people as so terrible; they might even think that *we* are at least partially responsible for the dispute. So we exaggerate: we describe the other person as having said more insulting things than they actually did, or as having acted toward us with far greater insensitivity or contempt than was the case. (Most of us are masters at attributing horrendous motives to people who have hurt us.) Our exaggerations, of which we ourselves might not be fully aware, are aimed at provoking others to validate and share our rage.

How productive is this "quick fix"? While almost all fights seem unavoidable when they happen, many turn out to be quite absurd or petty shortly thereafter. If we have made our anger known to many people, we might later find ourselves too embarrassed to make peace with our adversary, whom we have labeled thoroughly despicable. Alternatively, others may reach that conclusion—to our chagrin. As I once heard a young woman explain: "When I have a fight with my boyfriend, I never complain about him to my parents. Because even if I forgive him, my mother never will." All these are good reasons to be discreet when angry.

Furthermore, once an adversary hears what we are saying about him, he may become even more hostile than before. He may not only resist making peace but also start spreading his account of the dispute, in which we will undoubtedly emerge as considerably less heroic and victimized. Thus, a dispute can initiate a whole cycle of injury.

My advice, particularly if the matter is trivial, is to keep your anger to yourself; left alone, it may soon dissipate. Better yet, confront the person who hurt you. (Before doing so, it might be wise to hold back for a few days, containing your angry response while you try to see the matter in a broader perspective.) Assuming that your adversary is not a terrible individual (she likely is not if you have been on friendly terms until now), you could tell her: "You hurt me by saying or doing this . . ." or, "I think it was unfair of you to . . ." This might actually lead to an apology and a reconciliation. Ironically, sometimes we don't confront someone with whom we are angry because we don't wish to hear an explanation for her behavior, lest it deprive us of the self-righteous pleasure of our rage.

Of course, it's not always possible to confront the person who has angered you. If you confront an unfair boss, for example, you might risk losing your job. With a family member or in-law, a confrontation might provoke an escalation of tensions or even an irrevocable break. In such cases, it may be helpful to vent your anger to someone else, provided that you choose a confidant who will calm rather than incite you. (On the importance of feeling free to say whatever you're feeling to a therapist, see page 88.) Most of the time, however, gossiping merely intensifies the dispute and lessens the chances of reconciliation. (That is why, when you are the listener, you should try to be a calming influence rather than fan the flames of the offended one's anger.)

Making a conscious effort to speak ethically can help us become more emotionally direct and responsible and less likely to relate petty arguments to large numbers of people; we will learn, rather, to directly confront those whom we feel have mistreated us. Instead of being hapless victims, we come to view ourselves as capable of defending our own interests. This is no small advantage to be gained from undertaking to speak ethically.

IF YOU ARE GOING TO GOSSIP ANYWAY: TWO GUIDELINES

The preceding section describes just a few of the reasons we speak ill of others. Here we begin by noting that certainly not all gossip is motivated by the wish to do harm. Human behavior is fascinating, and generally anything that intrigues us is something we desire to share with others. Even the Talmud, the source of most of Judaism's laws of ethical speech, acknowledges that the large majority of people violate these laws at least once a day.[8]

What, then, should you do if it is difficult, perhaps impossible, always to refrain from speaking "negative truths" about others?

I suggest first that you severely limit the number of people with whom you gossip (and severely limit the amount of time you spend in such talk). If you or your partner learn something unusual, possibly negative, about a mutual friend, you will probably relate it to each other, and perhaps to one or two close friends. But be careful to stop there.

This is not an ideal solution, since your close friends may also share the information with close friends of theirs.

My friend Dennis Prager, the essayist and talk show host, argues that forbidding people to transmit any and all negative information or opinions about others is not only unrealistic but possibly also undesirable. Dennis once asked me, within the context of a conversation we were having about the troubled marriage of a mutual friend, "How can you say you care about someone and never talk about them?" Furthermore, he argued, "if you never speak about people with your partner, you're probably not very intimate with each other."

I know a woman whose husband almost never spoke about other people to her. She finally said to him, with some exasperation, "So what are we supposed to speak about all the time—the dangers of nuclear reactors and the latest actions of the mayor?" People who are close generally talk to each other about the people in their lives.

Therefore, here's a suggestion: if you're going to gossip (with a small number of people), develop a way of talking about others that is as kind and fair as you would want others to be when saying things about you that, though true, are not complimentary.

CHAPTER 4

Is It Ever Appropriate to Reveal Humiliating or Harmful Information About Another?

You shall not stand by while your brother's blood is shed.
—Leviticus 19:16

JEWISH LAW COMPARES spreading humiliating or harmful information to shedding blood, an act that is normally wrong, though not always (for example, killing in self-defense).

One specific case in which you are permitted to transmit "negative truths" is when you are asked for a business or job reference. As the Haffetz Hayyim (1838–1933), the Eastern European rabbinic sage who was Judaism's preeminent authority on the laws of permitted and forbidden speech, teaches: "If a person wants to take someone into his affairs—for example, to hire him in his business, or go into partnership with him . . . it is permitted for him to go around and ask and inquire from others . . . so as to prevent possible loss to himself. And it is permissible for others to reveal even very derogatory information, since the intent is not to harm the prospective employee, but to tell the truth in order to save one's fellow human being from potential harm."[1] Similarly, Jewish law insists that you speak frankly when someone requests your opinion about a prospective employee whom you know to be dishonest or incompetent.

Another instance in which revealing negative information is permitted is when someone is romantically involved with a person whom you know to be inappropriate or who is concealing information to which the partner is entitled.

In an important overview of Jewish perspectives on privacy, the Jewish legal scholar Rabbi Alfred S. Cohen tells of a young man whose friend was seriously dating his neighbor. The man knew that his friend had a serious health problem, and he realized from conversations with the young woman that she was unaware of his condition. He asked Rabbi Cohen whether he should disclose this fact to her, or whether this would constitute a violation of Judaism's laws forbidding gossip.[2]

The rabbi ruled that Jewish law *obliged* the young man to pass on this information to the woman, since she had the right to know about her boyfriend's medical condition before deciding whether or not to marry him. But, Rabbi Cohen noted, there is no clear-cut moral or legal guideline about *when* to transmit such information. If the man went around telling every woman whom his friend dated about his illness, his friend's social life would be ruined (as would their friendship). On the other hand, a woman who learns such information *after* she has gotten to know the man's more positive aspects will be in a far better position to judge the illness's significance for herself.

Morally, the best course would be for the young man to emphasize to his friend that he has a moral obligation to inform his partner himself, and that if he doesn't do so, he, the friend, will feel obliged to do so. Only in a case where someone won't give their romantic partner important information and the relationship is clearly serious should another person convey this information to the partner.[3] Presumably, the same advice would apply if you knew that a person had been unfaithful in a previous marriage, possessed a very bad temper, or was verbally or physically violent. This is information to which a would-be spouse is entitled.

Even in instances when you're permitted to share negative information, you should only reveal that which is *relevant*. Thus, if somebody inquires whether B would make a suitable business partner, you may—indeed *should*—say that B cheated a previous partner or came to work every day at 11 A.M. in a previous job and went home at 3 P.M. You should not, however, dredge up a fascinating but irrelevant scandal involving B's marriage.

When disclosing negative information, you should tell precisely what you know and nothing more. If you exaggerate, you are guilty of slander; in such a case, it would be morally preferable to say nothing at all.

You also should not disseminate embarrassing or negative information about a person to anyone besides those who need it. Otherwise moral people frequently violate this principle. They try to justify spreading negative news to large numbers of people by claiming that some who hear it might need it in the future. For example, everyone needs to know the reason a person's marriage broke up, since someone who hears the story might someday date him or her.

Occasionally, it *is* morally appropriate to share negative information with many people—for example, if a political candidate has misused his office for personal profit, or a physician is engaging in treatments that are harmful to patients, or an employer has sexually harassed his employees. In such cases, there may be many people who need this information—to vote against the dishonest politician, to avoid the unscrupulous doctor, or to avoid working for the abusive boss.

Follow this guiding principle for disseminating negative information: Will the information's recipient suffer from a "clear and present danger"—and it certainly need not be a life-threatening one—if he or she doesn't possess these facts?

As noted in chapter 2, if you are uncertain about the veracity of what you are passing along, then you must say so. In such a case, you are permitted to warn an inquiring would-be business partner, employer, employee, or potential mate to look into a specific matter, but you must explain that this information is either what you *heard* said (including why you think it might be credible) or something that you *suspect*. In the latter case, you must explain your suspicions and give the other person a chance to assess your reasoning (which he or she may find flimsy). A simple guideline: if you would not be prepared to swear under oath that a story is true, don't present it as undeniably true.

SHOULD CONFIDENCES EVER BE BROKEN?

What about deep, dark secrets confided to a cleric or a psychiatrist? Is it ever appropriate to reveal them? Here the ethical standards of the world and of different religions vary.

Consider an elementary or high school psychologist who learns that a student is using illegal drugs. Should the psychologist inform the child's parents? Over the years, I have posed this question before dozens of audiences. I have generally found that a large majority of listeners feel that the parents should be informed. Since they know that I am a rabbi, when I ask them what they think Jewish law would rule, an even larger majority express the conviction that it would *insist* that the parents be informed.

In fact, it is likely that Jewish law would take the opposite view. As Rabbi Alfred Cohen argues, involving the parents might ultimately prove beneficial to the child, but the disclosure of confidential information "might effectively stop other students from confiding in that psychologist and thereby prevent their being treated at all. Furthermore, if psychologists could not be trusted to maintain silence, people in general would stop using them. So the question really is, do psychologists benefit society as a whole? Will divulging secrets endanger the practice of that profession? What would be the net result to society if troubled persons no longer had someone to help them cope with personal problems?"[4]

This is a perfect example of the moral difficulties that ensue when an individual good clashes with a societal good. In this case, the rabbi suggests that the larger good of society constitutes a higher value than the possible benefit to one individual.

On the other hand, if the psychologist had good reason to believe that the boy's survival depended on his parents' knowing certain information (as in the case of a child contemplating suicide), ethics would dictate a different ruling.

Consider the tragic case of Tatiana Tarasoff, a University of California at Berkeley student who was murdered by a man named Prosenjit Poddar because she had rebuffed his romantic advances. After his arrest, it was revealed that Poddar had confided to his university-affiliated psychologist his intention to kill Tarasoff when she returned from her summer vacation. The psychologist had taken Poddar's threats so seriously that he informed campus police, who in turn detained Poddar for questioning. However, they released him when he appeared to be acting rationally. At that point, the psychologist's supervisor, also a psychologist, directed him to desist from further action regarding the case; as a result, Poddar's psychologist never contacted Tarasoff to warn her about the danger.

Unaware of what Poddar had confided to his psychologist, the Tarasoff family maintained a cordial relationship with the spurned suitor. Poddar even persuaded Tarasoff's brother to share an apartment with him and thus was in a position to learn when she returned from her vacation—at which time he murdered her.

Tarasoff's parents successfully sued the two university psychologists, as well as the University of California, for concealing this life-threatening information from the people most in need of it (their daughter and them). The majority of judges ruled that while doctor-patient confidentiality normally must be safeguarded, this privileged relationship should be breached when it puts an innocent person in serious danger.

Yet even so commonsensical a conclusion provoked the ire of dissenting justice William Clark, who argued that the doctor had acted appropriately in not contacting Tarasoff. Because of the majority ruling, he maintained, patients henceforth would fear that information confided to therapists, including threats, might be disclosed, and thus treatment of the mentally ill would be greatly impaired.[5]

Even if one rejects Justice Clark's premise—as I do—that it is preferable to sometimes let an innocent person die rather than violate a patient's confidence, the majority ruling in the Tarasoff case still leaves an open question: How can we reconcile our need, and society's, to have outlets for unacceptable feelings with the need to protect the objects of those feelings? Since many people confide fantasies of violence against other people to their therapists, when should a mental health professional disclose these threats to a potential victim and to the police? *Always* disclosing threats would hardly be realistic—or desirable. Many, if not most, of us have probably exclaimed at some point in our lives: "I could kill him! I really could!" It is usually perfectly clear to both the listener and the speaker that the threat is not intended seriously. So if a therapist has strong reason to believe that the patient is just venting his feelings, then clearly the patient-therapist confidence should not be broken. It would be very different, however, if a patient spoke to a therapist, for example, about shooting up a school (which has happened often in the United States, with fatal consequences). In such a case, we would want the therapist—and not just a therapist but anyone else privy to such information—to go to the proper authorities and tell them about this person who might well be a walking time bomb.

Does this guideline place an unfair burden on the therapist, forcing her to decide case by case whether a threat is seriously intended?

In truth, this guideline does place a difficult responsibility on the therapist. Perhaps the therapist's best way to assess such threats is to personalize them—to imagine that the violent sentiments are directed toward him- or herself or toward a loved one. If the therapist feels no trepidation about the threat, then it is very likely— though not certainly—inconsequential. On the other hand, if the therapist feels fearful when personalizing the threat (knowing that she would tell her spouse and children, "If you ever see this person come to the house, don't let him in"), she should be morally obliged to inform the potential victim and the authorities. If personalizing a threat makes it seem more potent to the therapist, so be it. If an error must be made, better it should be made in the direction of saving an innocent life rather than safeguarding a would-be murderer's privacy.[6]

The doctor should also ask himself what he would do if a patient speaks of committing suicide and the threat seems to be serious. Would he break the rules of confidentiality and tell members of the patient's family, or any other relevant person, in order to protect the patient? And if he would, then should he not, by the same token, warn people whom the patient might harm?

Are the ethics different in the case of clergy-client confidentiality? For example, there is a well-known Catholic canon law that prohibits revelations of any statements made in confession, even when a life is at stake.

Not surprisingly, so uncompromising a position can lead to great moral difficulties. In Alfred Hitchcock's classic film *I Confess*, a man confesses to a priest that he murdered someone, then plants circumstantial evidence implicating the cleric. Although the priest is aware of the killer's identity, he finds himself forbidden to disclose it to the police, even after he becomes the prime suspect, and even after an innocent woman's reputation is destroyed during a thorough and somewhat mean-spirited police investigation.[7]

A similar dilemma lies at the heart of Father William Kienzle's best-selling murder mystery *The Rosary Murders*. Here a serial killer confesses his crime to a priest and tells him the reason for his actions.[8] Unlike his counterpart in *I Confess*, the priest doesn't know the anonymous confessor's identity. But he too acknowledges and accepts that Catholic law prohibits him from informing the police about the confession, or any details he learned during it, lest this information enable them to identify the killer. After painful soul-searching—the thought of innocent people dying bothers him terribly—he concludes: "Should protecting the seal [of confession] cost a priest his life, or another innocent life, no reason was sufficient, no cause important enough to violate that seal."[9] (In the novel, the priest ends up solving the murder himself.)

Jewish law is far less categorical. A case that tested the principle of rabbi-client confidentiality occurred in New York some years ago. A short time after a married woman was murdered, her husband sought out a prominent rabbinic scholar and confessed to being haunted by his wife's death—though he was unsure whether the murder in his mind was a real memory or a dream. During the meeting, it became clear to the rabbi that the man was speaking about himself. Afterward, the rabbi went to the police. Their investigation revealed that the husband, who was deeply in debt, had taken out a large life insurance policy on his wife shortly before she was murdered. After the man was arrested, the rabbi testified as a prosecution witness at his trial, and the man was convicted of the murder of his wife.

At the time, some members of the Jewish community felt that the rabbi had acted unjustly; they felt that, at the very least, he should have informed the killer that his disclosures would not be held in confidence. This objection seems unreasonable, given the husband's violent nature and the rabbi's natural fear of the harm the man might do to protect his terrible secret.

Then, too, an important biblical principle states: "Do not stand by while your neighbor's blood is shed" (Leviticus 19:16), which Jewish law understands as a mandate not to withhold help or information that could be of life-and-death significance to another person. Important as confidentiality is, it is a less compelling value than saving a person's life and/or bringing a killer to justice (and making sure thereby that the killer can never kill again).

While people generally have the right to expect a doctor, psychologist, clergyperson, or lawyer to safeguard their secrets, this right, at least as I understand it, should be canceled when a higher good, the protection of innocent life, is at stake.*

---

* I understand that canon law, as it has been explained to me, seems to differ with my conclusion.

CHAPTER 5

Privacy and Public Figures

SO FAR, WE have discussed the rights of ordinary people to have their privacy respected. But what about public figures, especially those we have entrusted with the power to lead us? Are they a special case, or do we have the same ethical obligations toward them?

Many journalists consider public figures to be a special case. As the late Howard Simons, a managing editor of the *Washington Post* and a prominent proponent of this view, put it: "I don't believe any politician in the United States ought to have a private life."[1]

Those who share this view argue that *any* activity in which a person engages can reveal significant information about his or her character; thus, the voting public has the right to know it all. This belief is now so ingrained in the American psyche that many people rarely question, on either moral or practical grounds, the assertion that anyone who enters public life loses the right to protect himself from all public scrutiny.

Yet is it moral to deny any human being, including a public official, a sphere of privacy in which she can act without fear that her actions will be reported to large numbers of people?

The answer is no. It is morally unjustifiable—at least as I understand it—to deny public officials a private life. As the professor of philosophy David Nyberg writes in *The Varnished Truth*: "A life without privacy is unthinkable. How could we make love? Reflect or meditate? Write a poem, keep a diary . . . attend to those sometimes highly self-conscious requirements of skin and bowels? . . . Civility itself requires privacy."[2]

But don't such no-holds-barred investigations lead voters to select better-qualified, more ethical candidates? Isn't the evil of even intrusive snooping outweighed by a greater good? Again I would answer no. Forty years of muckraking, much of it centered on candidates' private lives, does not seem to have led to the election of more capable or more honest people.* Indeed, one of the primary achievements of this muckraking has been to make Americans more cynical and less trusting than ever of their elected leaders.[3] (It has also, as shall be discussed, caused no shortage of sensitive and highly ethical people to shy away from entering public life.)

One feature of what the political scientist Larry Sabato labels "attack journalism" is extensive coverage of public figures' sexual indiscretions and misbehaviors, a subject that arouses the greatest amount of popular and journalistic obsession.[4] Yet no evidence suggests that presidents (or other public officials and opinionmakers) who have engaged in extramarital affairs have proven less effective or, more important, less trustworthy than those who have not.

Americans have paid a steep price for the media's ongoing obsession with sexual gossip. Most important, it has caused media attention to focus on personal rather than substantive issues. The reporter Steven Roberts has observed that "more ink was devoted [in the 1970s] to Congressman Wilbur Mills' exploits with Fanne F. [a stripper with whom the congressman had had an affair] than to

---

* Obviously, I am not talking about people who have engaged in criminal behavior, which they have no right to conceal.

Wilbur Mills' writing half the tax laws on the books. Does that serve the readers and make sense? Not to me."5

While Roberts is correct that this focus on the personal makes no logical sense, the reason for the media's skewed priorities is clear to anyone who understands human nature. People are more interested in erotic matters than they are in substantive issues. Ask most voters to prioritize a set of issues in terms of the national interest, and sexual behavior will rank near the bottom. Announce, however, that a television program investigating a candidate's love life—including problematic relationships and potential scandals—will be broadcast at the same time as a program discussing the candidate's positions on some of the most pressing issues facing America, including economic and security issues, and which program do you think will attract more viewers?

The question is rhetorical, and not because viewers have deluded themselves into thinking that this topic is more important, but because it interests them more.

Most of us are very interested in others' failings, particularly their sexual peccadilloes. Even when we acknowledge that such curiosity is intrusive, uncouth, and even immoral, it is difficult to suppress it. (If you were in a friend's house, walked into the bedroom, found your friend's diary open, and saw the words "I had sex yesterday with . . . ," would you have the moral strength and character to close the diary?)

Early in the 1988 presidential campaign, the *Miami Herald* reported that there was strong circumstantial evidence that a senator who was a leading contender for a major party nomination was having a sexual affair, and he was forced to withdraw from the race. (I am not mentioning either the man's or the woman's name as both of them have suffered greatly for their behavior and are, I suspect, happy to be out of the public eye.)

The case received a tremendous amount of publicity at the time, and over the years I have asked dozens of audiences: "How many of you think that the public had the right to know about this relationship and presumed affair?" Regularly, between 10 and 20 percent say yes, the public had the right to know, while well over 60 percent say no.

I address my next question only to the "no" majority: "As an outgrowth of your belief that the public had no right to this knowledge, how many of you refused to read articles about the supposed affair and turned off your television sets when it was announced that pictures were now going to be shown of the woman with whom the candidate had his relationship?" Almost everyone laughs at this question and, at most, one or two hands go up.

Those who believe that the public had no moral right to know about this presumed affair but who followed the case avidly are not hypocrites; they are human beings with normal human interests. Almost all negative gossip, particularly about sex, is so inherently interesting that it is very hard to ignore. To draw an analogy, most married Americans believe in monogamy. But if every time they checked into a hotel, a very attractive person were waiting for them in their room, many "confirmed" monogamists would commit adultery. Mercifully, few of us are presented with such temptations.

Perhaps the most unfortunate repercussion of the media's obsession with the private lives of public figures is that it has caused Americans to pay less attention to far more substantive and significant issues.

IN ADDITION TO criminal acts, such as sexual offenses, accepting bribes, embezzling funds, and the like, the chief offense for which public officials deserve to be called to account is hypocrisy. For example, does the person engage in conduct he denounces or wishes to see punished in others? If not, then great caution is advised. A few years back, a friend of mine whose husband holds a high public office called me for advice about an ethical dilemma. She and her husband had learned that a prominent adversary of her husband's political party once conducted an adulterous affair. His mistress had become pregnant, and the man urged her to have an abortion. She did, and he paid for it.

Both of us knew that revealing such information would definitely end the man's political career, given that he had carefully cultivated an image of great moral rectitude. I asked my friend only one question: Did this man currently oppose the right of women to have abortions? If yes, his hypocrisy in arranging an abortion when it suited his interests would be so clear that it seemed to me that this information should be released.

But if he supported a woman's right to have an abortion, I believed that "outing" him for having committed adultery would be immoral: the man's relationship with his wife was intact, and the woman with whom he had an affair had gone on with her life, and it was only by the strangest of coincidences that this information had come into my friend's hands.

My friend acknowledged that the adversary supported abortion rights but cited other political stances with which she disagreed, positions on which I concurred with her. However, I maintained that it would be indefensible to reveal his infidelity and the abortion. Much as we may dislike somebody, to dig up and disseminate whatever "dirt" we can to destroy him or her would still be wrong.

Of course, everything I have written about until now involves consensual relations. It does not apply to someone who uses their position of authority to pressure a person into sexual relations—

particularly a person dependent on them for employment. (For example, Harvey Weinstein, one of Hollywood's most successful and acclaimed producers, engaged in crude, vile, and most likely criminal behavior and also apparently harmed the careers of some of the actresses who refused his sexual demands.) A person who engages in such behavior puts himself outside the protection of the laws of *lashon ha-ra*. Pretty much anyone around him—and certainly women who have dealings with him—are at risk and have the right to be forewarned.

But aside from instances like these, public figures should not be exempt from the right to privacy that we all enjoy. Except for those aspects of their lives that relate to job performance, they should be able to keep their private lives private. Ironically, the obsession with invading our leaders' private lives has not even achieved the one good one might expect: a deeper knowledge of those whose lives have been investigated. Because candidates are aware that the media treat them like arrested felons ("Anything you say can be used against you"), many confine themselves to banalities when speaking in the presence of journalists. They not inappropriately assume that it's safer to appear bland than to risk making a personal revelation or issuing a statement that could be cited out of context and used to damn them in the future.

Finally, it's likely that such intrusive scrutiny discourages many Americans, some with fine characters, from considering public service. How many among us, if nominated to a political position that would provoke our ideological opponents to ask everyone who has known us, "Tell us the worst thing you know about so-and-so, or the worst thing you have ever heard about him, and tell us the names of anybody you know who dislikes him, so we can speak to them," would willingly undergo such scrutiny, however moral our lives?

Even journalists bent on exposing every public figure's feet of clay do not wish to sustain such an indignity. Some years ago, Paul Taylor, a *Washington Post* reporter, asked the straying presidential candidate referred to earlier whether he thought that adultery was immoral. When the candidate said yes, Taylor asked him if he had committed adultery. After a moment's stammering, the candidate responded: "I don't have to answer that." A few weeks later, after the man had withdrawn from the presidential campaign, *People* magazine posed to Taylor the same two questions he had addressed to the candidate. "Yes, I do consider adultery immoral," the journalist responded. "The answer to the second question is 'None of your business.'"[6]

In other words, even those who spread gossip don't want to be its victims. Indeed, many journalists routinely declare their own lives off limits, even when one could make a case that the public has a legitimate right to know about them. For example, journalists who cover the U.S. Congress or the White House seldom say what their political preferences are or which candidate they hope wins. Sometimes the newspapers that employ them do not permit them to be members of a political party or to vote in elections, but that doesn't prevent journalists from having political preferences. Cannot an argument be made that the public should have the right to know if someone reporting a scandal or other negative information about a candidate or nominee has personally favored—perhaps strongly favored—that candidate's opponent? Couldn't the public then better assess whether the journalist similarly reports negative information about the candidate or party he or she favors?

Perhaps the worst repercussion of "attack journalism" is that some decent people, precisely because they are more easily ashamed, have been and will be discouraged from entering the public arena. The late *New York Times* columnist Anthony Lewis argued, quite persuasively I think, that "if we tell people there's to be absolutely nothing private left to them, then we will tend to attract to public office only those most brazen, least sensitive personalities."[7]

Surely such an outcome serves no moral good. The time has come to return to some of the civility that prevailed in the past.

PART THREE

HOW WE SPEAK TO OTHERS

CHAPTER 6

Controlling Rage and Anger

Only God can give us credit for the angry words we did not speak.

—Rabbi Harold Kushner

THE BIBLE ALMOST always describes romantic love from the male's perspective. We are told that Isaac loved Rebecca (Genesis 24:67), Jacob loved Rachel (Genesis 29:18), and Samson, with far less happy results, loved Delilah (Judges 16:4). In the entire Bible, there is only one woman whose love for a man is recorded: "Now Michal, daughter of [King] Saul loved David" (I Samuel 18:20). A short time later, when Michal's father, afraid that David will usurp the throne, plots to kill him, she helps David escape by lowering him from a window. She then confuses the hired assassins by placing a human image, topped with hair and dressed in clothes, in David's bed (I Samuel 19:11–17). By the time the would-be killers realize Michal's ruse, her beloved is far away.

Although the Bible never reports that David reciprocated Michal's love, we do know that he risked his life in one-on-one battles with two hundred Philistines to win Michal's hand in marriage (I Samuel 18:25–29). Later, when David spent years hiding from King Saul, Saul gave Michal, still David's wife, to a man named

Phalti. Although many husbands would have repudiated a wife who had acquiesced to such an arrangement, when David became king, he restored Michal as his queen.

Yet, despite the intense love at their relationship's outset, David and Michal's marriage becomes perhaps the saddest in the Bible. Within a few years, this once-devoted couple are totally estranged. David and Michal both suffer from the same character flaw—a sharp tongue, which each refuses to control when angry. The Bible describes the incident that triggers the end of their love. Ironically, it happens at a celebration: David is supervising the return to Jerusalem of the Ark of the Lord, the holiest object in ancient Jewish life. The Ark, which contains the Ten Commandments, was captured by the Philistines many years earlier. In an outburst of joy, David dances passionately, even wildly, in front of thousands of his subjects. Watching the whole scene from a palace window, Michal is disgusted by the spectacle of a monarch carrying on with such abandon. And so when David returns to the palace, she greets him with cold sarcasm: "Didn't the king of Israel do himself honor today—exposing himself . . . as one of the riffraff might expose himself?" (II Samuel 6:20).

Are Michal's withering remarks justified? Has David truly acted in a manner that diminishes the dignity of his office? Perhaps, but whether or not Michal is right, her tactless criticism of her husband on this great day in his life blows a dispute into a gale-force fury.

Michal's attack, however, is only the first factor in the tragedy that ensues. In the face of his wife's scorn, David does not remain silent, walk away until the tension eases, or even try to defend his behavior. Instead, he responds with the cruelest counterattack he can muster: "It was before the Lord Who chose me instead of your father and all his family [that I danced]" (II Samuel 6:21).

David's words in no way address the substance of Michal's critique. As many of us do when criticized, he goes "straight for blood," attacking the most painful event in Michal's life, God's rejection of her father and his subsequent death, along with three of Michal's brothers, at the hands of the Philistines.

In the very next verse, the Bible records: "So to her dying day Michal, daughter of Saul, had no children." Why is Michal's childlessness recorded at this point? Perhaps because after so brutal an exchange—and there might well have been others—Michal and David were never again intimate.

The Bible's point is as clear today as it was in 1000 BCE: if a husband or wife, or two siblings or friends, do not restrain their words when they are angry, love is unlikely to survive, *no matter how deeply the two people once cared for each other.* The ability to control what we say when we're angry is a prerequisite for a lasting relationship.

Unfortunately, this piece of biblical wisdom flies in the face of much modern thinking. Today many people believe that it's unhealthy to suppress rage. If you feel an emotion, it's considered important to express exactly what you're feeling.

To which I ask, "Why?"

That you feel rage does not entitle you to inflict emotional pain on others any more than feelings of sexual attraction entitle you to harass the source of your attraction.

Some might argue that, unlike sexual harassment, rage is sometimes justifiable. And sometimes, though not often, it is. But then again, what angry person doesn't feel that his or her rage is justified? One of anger's insidious qualities is how easy it is to find a thousand excuses for it. And while rage sometimes is justified—what other emotion should one feel toward an Adolf Eichmann or a Charles Manson?—many of us express rage not when it's justified but when only far milder emotions are warranted.

As the psychotherapist Bernie Zilbergeld has written: "I cannot count the number of times that married couples tell me, 'I've got all this anger bottled up and I need to get it out.' Sure you do, and I'll be happy to cater the divorce."

Even when anger is justified, it is unfair, unjust, and hence morally wrong to express it in ways disproportionate to the provocation.

So what if you find it painful to hold in your angry feelings? Isn't it morally preferable that you experience the pain of suppressing disproportionate or out-of-control anger rather than make the person with whom you're angry experience the pain of being on the receiving end?

Rage is not only destructive (as in the case of David and Michal) but also *self*-destructive. The Rabbis claim that when a wise man loses control of his temper, his wisdom deserts him. Thus, the book of Numbers describes an episode in which Moses becomes outraged at the Israelites' incessant whining about water—and pretty much about everything. God directs him to speak to a large rock, from which He will then send water to satisfy the people's thirst. But Moses, still furious at the Israelites' many years of complaining, disobeys God's command. Instead of speaking to the rock, Moses strikes it, saying, "Listen, you rebels, shall we get water for you out of this rock?" (Numbers 20:10).

Many of us hit objects when we're angry. The Torah's point is profound: when angry, you should attempt to speak, not hit or burst out in rage. Furthermore, when we're angry, we are apt to make extreme and unwise comments. Thus, although Moses surely did not intend it, his use of "we" implies that it is he and his brother Aaron (who is standing alongside him), not God, who are responsible for the miracle of the water gushing forth from the rock. That is a dangerously foolish comment, the kind we all make when angry, and it could have led the Israelites to believe that Moses himself was a god.[1] Moses pays dearly for his loss of self-control: God denies him entry into the Promised Land.

In addition to acting unwisely, we often *appear* foolish when we lose our temper. In his book *Acting in Film*, the actor Michael Caine recalls that

> *I used to lose my temper. I would fly off the handle quite quickly in a work situation. Then I worked on a picture called* The Last Valley *by James Clavell, who had been a prisoner of the Japanese during World War II. James looks like an Englishman, but he really thinks like a Japanese. I lost my temper one day, and James just looked at me and let me finish ranting and raving, and then he said, "Come with me, Mike. Let's go round the corner and sit down." He sat me down and talked to me about the Japanese theory of losing face. If you start to scream and shout, you look like a fool, and you feel like a fool, and you earn the disrespect of everyone. . . . I've never lost my temper in a work situation again.*[2]

A close friend of my wife, a man who has long struggled with his temper, once put it well: "Haven't you learned already that when you lose control of your temper, you look deranged, like a person taken over by animal rage?"

It is therefore important to control our rage, however "righteous" it may be. We may well have little control over what *provokes* our anger, *but all of us*, unless we are under the influence of mind-altering drugs, suffer some mental illness, or have certain types of brain damage, can almost always control how we express our anger.

The psychologist Richard Gelles tells of a marriage counselor who was interviewing a man who often physically abused his wife.

"'Why do you beat up your wife?' the counselor asked the husband.

"'I can't control myself,' the man responded. 'I just lose control.'

"The counselor, being a very wise person, asked: 'Well, why don't you shoot her or stab her?'

"The husband had no response to that because the only answer he could have given would be, 'I can't shoot or stab my wife, I might [permanently] hurt her.' [This man] knew very well what he was doing."[3]

If you believe that you truly can't control your temper, imagine the following scenario: You're walking along the street late at night when you are suddenly confronted by a mugger with a knife or gun who demands your money. I think it can be safely assumed that there are few people whom you would hate more than this thug. Yet do you express your rage? Do you curse the person? Not at all. Chances are you treat the person very politely and offer all the cash you have.

Of course, the only reason you do so is because you fear the person. But that is not the point. The point is that we can control our temper when we really want to.

To take another, less extreme, example. You and another person, say a family member, are having a screaming, no-holds-barred fight when suddenly the doorbell rings. Someone whom you're very eager to impress, such as a boss or a new client, stands in front of your door. Would you go on ranting or would you find a way to suppress your rage?[4]

Perhaps you would suppress your rage for a short while, for as long as it took until the visitor left, whereupon the fight would erupt again. But even if that happens, your ability to delay your rage means that you do have some control over your temper. Furthermore, the delay itself would probably lessen the fight's intensity. As the psychologist Carol Tavris cautions: "Expressing anger while you feel [most] angry nearly always makes you angrier."

I would go a step further. I believe that most of us can control the expression of anger for far longer than a few minutes or even a few hours. Here's another, admittedly highly unlikely, scenario: Suppose you were told that if you cut back on screaming or otherwise speaking harshly and expressing anger at your spouse (or children, or friends, or employees, or all the preceding) by 75 percent for six months, you would be given $2 million. Do you think you would find a way to control your temper?

I think most of us would become geniuses at learning how to control our anger.

In truth, almost every one of us has far more control over our rage than we are willing to acknowledge. For some the control might be almost total, while for others it might be far less. People who have less control must recognize their *moral* obligation to curb their harsh words. If they find themselves incapable of doing so on their own, they are *morally* obligated to seek the sort of professional help that will enable them to exert greater self-control.

Each year, large numbers of once-loving relationships worth far more than $2 million are destroyed because of the hateful things people say when angry. To counter this, we must destroy the myth that Michal and David, and you and I, cannot control what we say or do.

Dr. Stephen Marmer, a professor of psychiatry at the UCLA School of Medicine, recommends that in dealing with anger we think in terms of layers, or cascades, of control:

1. Control of our initial reaction

2. Control of our initial response

3. Control of our initial reaction to the other's response

4. Control of our succeeding reactions

Moving down this list, the degree of control grows progressively greater. Thus, even if you have not controlled your initial response, you can exert greater control over your next response and work to repair any damage you might have caused earlier. Indeed, one of the saddest things about the David-Michal story is that the Bible records no effort by either to repair the damage caused by their tactless and cruel words.

This is not to say that it is always wrong to feel anger or to express it, *within ethical limits*. When Maimonides, the preeminent medieval Jewish philosopher and rabbinic scholar, wrote on the need to control one's temper, he also warned that a person should not become so indifferent to what others do that he becomes like a corpse, totally incapable of feeling.[5] Maimonides's cautionary words might well have been in response to the extreme strictures expressed by some Roman thinkers against ever expressing anger. Seneca, the first-century Stoic philosopher, argued that people could control their tempers no matter what the provocation. He cited the story of Harpagus, who, instead of going into a rage when a Persian king presented him with the heads and flesh of his own children, responded bloodlessly: "At the king's board, any kind of food is delightful."[6]

What Maimonides proposes instead is an emotional golden mean: "[A person] should . . . display anger only when the matter is serious enough to warrant it, in order to prevent the matter from recurring."[7] In this regard, he might well have been influenced by the nuanced advice of Aristotle, of whom Maimonides was a lifelong student: "It is a slavish nature that will submit to being insulted or let friends be insulted unresistingly. . . . A person is praised who is angry for the right reasons, with the right people, and also in the right way, at the right time, and for the right length of time."[8]

Each of Aristotle's five conditions can help us guard against inappropriate expressions of anger:

For the right reasons: We should not become angry over petty matters.

With the right person: If we are angry at our boss, we should not come home and take it out on our spouse or children. Also, for example, at work we should not get upset at our supervisor for implementing an unfair order from our mutual boss, in what is known in popular parlance as "blaming the messenger" and in psychological terms as "displacement."

In the right way: Even when we are justifiably angry, we are still required to act fairly. If your anger is disproportionate to the provocation, then it is better not to express it at all, or to wait until you have calmed down before you speak of the matter. One way to assess whether your anger is excessive is to ask yourself—and this requires self-discipline—whether you still feel any concern or compassion for the person who has upset you. If the only emotion you can get in touch with is rage, then your anger is, most probably, excessive. The appeal of the prophet Habakkuk, directed to God, contains a reminder that applies to all of us when angry: "In Your wrath, remember mercy" (3:2; see also chapter 7 on fighting fairly).[9]

At the right time and for the right length of time: We shouldn't react immediately, unless we know we are calm. Right after something has enraged us, our anger may be out of control. It is better to wait until we are more composed. However, we also should not react long after the event has occurred, by which time the offending party may assume that all is normal and is shocked to learn that we have been harboring anger. Finally, we must learn to let go of our anger once we have expressed it. The cohesiveness of many families has been destroyed by members who hold on to their rage for years, or even decades.[10]

Aristotle's checklist is an important one for each of us to review when we are angry. Otherwise, we will not hold our anger in check, believing, even when we are wrong, that we are justified. The Catholic theologian St. Francis de Sales wrote that anger "is nourished by a thousand false pretexts; there never was an angry man who thought his anger unjust."*

IF YOU'VE EVER ruptured a close relationship with angry words, consider whether observing the following rule could have led to a different outcome: *Limit the expression of your anger to the incident that provoked it.* Focusing the discussion in this way avoids making the criticized party feel that his or her whole being is being attacked. It is this principle that David violated in his cruel counterattack after Michal mocked his dancing. He could have responded in many different ways: "I was overcome with joy, and I didn't want to rein in my dancing," or "I made myself more, not less, beloved in the eyes of the people by showing them that I am a creature of flesh and blood just like them." He could even have spoken more sharply: "You are the one who acted like a cold aristocrat, Michal, by behaving indifferently on so great a day."

However, what David did wrong was to attack Michal at her point of greatest vulnerability. "It was before the Lord Who chose me instead of your father and all his family [that I danced]." These words, by alluding to the most tragic event in Michal's life, were calculated to humiliate and devastate his wife; they were the equivalent of responding to a slap in the face with a shot to the heart.

---

* In modern times, the most obvious exemplars of such an attitude are terrorists, who justify the most heinous acts against innocent people.

Unfortunately, many people act as David did. In Somerset Maugham's *Of Human Bondage*, the protagonist, Philip, has a club-foot. One reason for Philip's generally low estimation of human nature is the realization "that when his fellows were angry with him, they never failed to taunt him with his deformity."

We all have "clubfeet." For Michal, it was the pain of her father's rejection by God. For someone else, it could be a weight problem, or a lack of professional success, or an unhappy love life. To bring another person's vulnerability into an argument is wrong. Absolutely wrong. If you ever become tempted to attack someone where he or she is most vulnerable, stop yourself from doing it as surely as you would stop yourself from punching a friend at whom you were upset. The worst time possible to allude to painful areas in another person's life is during a fight. You are likely to be much harsher, and the other person far less receptive, if he thinks your comments are part of an attack. If sore points must be discussed, do so when you are feeling love for the person, not animosity.

Had David and Michal abided by this rule, they could have fought about the issue that provoked their anger, but their dignity, and hence their relationship, could have remained intact.

Yet another reason words said when we are angry can cause such hurt and alienation is that people generally assume that what we say when we are angry is what we truly feel. And it *is* what we truly feel. At *that* moment. When we are angry, we often feel and think unfairly. Few of us would want our parents, spouses, children, or friends to know every angry thought about them that goes through our heads. That is why many of us choose to keep such thoughts to ourselves. But once we release these often distorted thoughts into the world, others tend to assume they represent our *true* feelings— not just our thoughts during those moments of rage.

Therefore, we should be guided by the words of Solomon ibn Gabirol, the eleventh-century Spanish Jewish philosopher and poet: "I can retract what I did not say, but I cannot retract what I have already said."

THE ONE PLACE WHERE IT IS APPROPRIATE TO EXPRESS YOUR ANGER

A therapist's office is exactly where you should say whatever you are feeling. Expressing your deepest anger will enable both you and the therapist to come to a better understanding of your needs and fears and may help you devise ways to exert better self-control. And because of the therapist's obligation to not transmit anything you say to anyone else (except in the rarest life-threatening circumstances; see pages 60–65), you need not be concerned that your possibly disproportionate and unfair comments will become known to the people with whom you are angry.

THE FLIP SIDE of expressing disproportionate anger is not expressing it at all. Many of us, when emotionally hurt, tend to withdraw from the person who has hurt us rather than address the issue. This withdrawal violates the following biblical injunction: "Do not hate your brother in your heart" (Leviticus 19:17).

When we learned this law as yeshiva students, my classmates and I found it unintentionally amusing. "Does that mean," one boy challenged our teacher, "that it's all right to hate somebody as long as you tell them to their face?"

"More or less," the rabbi answered, to our surprise. "Of course, it would be better if you don't hate somebody, but when you're angry at a person, you should confront him or her. Otherwise, your anger will fester and grow."

By way of example, he offered the biblical story of Joseph and his brothers. Their father, Jacob, has twelve sons, but he favors Joseph and makes no effort to disguise his favoritism. His father presents him with a special ornamental garment, "a coat of many colors," which he presents to Joseph alone and not to his siblings. Jacob also seems to encourage Joseph to tattle on his brothers, further inflaming their wrath. As the Bible tells us, "And Joseph brought bad reports of [his brothers] to their father" (Genesis 37:2). In addition, Joseph antagonizes his brothers by telling them of his dreams predicting that one day they will all bow down to him.

What is the effect of all these interactions? "They hated him so that they could not speak a friendly word to him" (a more literal rendering of this verse might yield the translation "so that they couldn't speak peaceably to him").

We don't know how long the silent treatment and the suppressed rage go on, but apparently it's a good while. It also sets the stage for the brothers' total eruption when they are away from home on a work trip and see Joseph—dispatched by Jacob to check up on how they are doing—coming toward them in his fancy garment. After debating whether or not to kill him, they decide to sell him into Egyptian slavery and then trick their father into thinking Joseph has been killed by a wild beast (for more on this episode, see page 125).

Our teacher then reminded us of yet another instance in which a person didn't express his anger, but let it fester. The Bible relates the story of two half-brothers, Amnon and Absalom, both sons of King David. In one of the Bible's unhappiest episodes, Amnon rapes and then abandons Absalom's sister Tamar (who is Amnon's half-sister). Afterward, Absalom never confronts his brother: "And Absalom spoke to Amnon neither good nor evil for Absalom hated Amnon" (II Samuel 13:22). Ultimately he arranges, two years later, to have Amnon killed.

Whether or not Amnon deserved to die is beside the point, the teacher told us. Rather, we should note the Bible's words: "And Absalom spoke to Amnon neither good nor evil for Absalom hated Amnon." It is deduced from this that a person who remains unnaturally silent when an expression of anger is called for might later explode in murderous rage.

Of course, most of us suffer much less grievous provocations and, rather than overreacting to them by killing someone, we nurse our injuries in silence, talk about them to people who cannot help, or inflict our anger on innocent people. As the psychologist Carol Tavris has written:

> If you are angry at Ludwig, all the discussions in the world with your best friend will not solve the problem. Unless the discussions result in your changing your perception of Ludwig ("Oh, I hadn't realized he didn't mean to insult me") it is likely to reinforce your own interpretations, with the result that you rehearse your anger rather than ridding yourself of it. If you displace your anger by punching pillows, conjuring up vengeful scenarios, telling nasty jokes or hitting your child, your anger will not be diminished nor will the displacement be cathartic. This is because the cause of your anger remains unchanged.[11]

When you are angry, remember that there will always be time to break irrevocably with your antagonist. Sharing your anger with many other people might prematurely cause such a break.

If you do speak about the matter with others, choose people who might calm you down and help you to see things in a broader, less bitter perspective. Avoid those who are apt to provoke your rage ("He said *that* to you? That's disgusting! What are you going to do about it?"). But most important, try to speak to the person with whom you are angry; more often than you might think, they may

not realize that they have hurt you, or that they hurt you so griev-
ously, and they might well apologize and be truly repentant.

Directing our attention to the object of our anger underscores the
importance of direct communication between antagonistic parties.
A rabbi I know in Los Angeles received a letter from a congregant
who was unhappy about a certain development in the synagogue.
The rabbi knew that the policy that had offended his correspondent
had been established well before his arrival as the synagogue's spiritual leader. He showed the letter to the synagogue's president, who
told him that he would personally draft a response and explain the
policy to the unhappy congregant.

There the matter ended—or so the rabbi thought. Sometime
later, the synagogue president received a letter from the congregant,
who explained that since the rabbi hadn't responded to his letter,
he felt that he had no spiritual leader in the congregation and was
resigning his membership. He also noted that when the congregation engaged a new rabbi, he would be willing to rejoin. In addition
to asking that his letter be shared with the whole board, he sent the
rabbi a copy.

The rabbi described to me his reaction when he read the congregant's letter: "All sorts of angry thoughts ran through my mind. I
felt like writing him, 'I am sorry that I drove as kind a man as you
to write such ugly things. Furthermore, your need to suggest that
my dying, resigning or being fired would prompt your return to the
synagogue was gratuitously nasty.'"

Of course, he wrote no such thing. Upset though he was, he wisely
read the congregant's letter to a fellow rabbi. When he finished, his
colleague offered a surprising response: "The way this man phrased
his letter was definitely angering. But with all due respect, you are
not fully in the right either. The letter was addressed to you and, seeing how upset he was, you should have responded, if only to tell him
that he would be hearing from the president."

The rabbi swallowed hard and remained silent for a while. "You're right," he finally said to his colleague. "Well, if the right is not all on my side, then why am I feeling so annoyed at this man?"

He thought about this question a while longer, and finally realized that had the complainant written him a second time, telling him how upset he was not to have received a response to his letter, he would have felt terrible. He would have been horrified to realize that he had hurt someone deeply and would immediately have called or written the man.

Instead, the congregant had never informed him of his hurt and anger. Rather, he had shared his angry feelings with the rabbi's employers, the synagogue's board of directors, hoping thereby to inflame other people against him and to bring about his dismissal. Thus, instead of being able to think clearly about the possible legitimacy of the man's critique, the rabbi responded with fury.

Much wisdom still inheres in William Blake's old quatrain:

I was angry with my friend:
I told my wrath, my wrath did end.
I was angry with my foe:
I told it not, my wrath did grow.

CHAPTER 7

Fighting Fairly

ONE DAY, RESH Lakish, a young man who was a gladiator and a bandit, saw Rabbi Yochanan, the leading scholar of his age, bathing in the Jordan. The young gladiator jumped in after him, and the two began to speak. Impressed with Resh Lakish's physical appearance and obvious intelligence, Rabbi Yochanan said to him, "Strength like yours should be devoted to Torah."

Resh Lakish countered by saying: "Good looks like yours should be devoted to women," for Rabbi Yochanan was an unusually handsome man.

"If you will repent," Rabbi Yochanan answered, "I will arrange for you to marry my sister. She is even better-looking than I."

When Resh Lakish agreed, Rabbi Yochanan arranged the marriage; he also became Resh Lakish's tutor. Within a few years, the ex-gladiator and bandit became one of Israel's leading scholars.

Sometime later, an argument arose in Rabbi Yochanan's yeshiva. The dispute was of a highly technical nature, focusing on the point during production when different items become susceptible to ritual impurity. Rabbi Yochanan argued that metallic objects such as swords, knives, and daggers are considered fully formed—and therefore susceptible to ritual impurity—only at the moment a smith hardens them in a furnace.

Disagreeing, Resh Lakish contended that they can only be judged completed at the moment the smith dips them in cold water.

Annoyed at being publicly challenged, Rabbi Yochanan sarcastically responded: "A robber understands his trade."

Stung by Yochanan's allusion to his disreputable past, Resh Lakish countered: "What good, then, have you done me by influencing me to give up my life as a bandit? Among the gladiators I was called 'Master,' and here too, I am called 'Master.'"

"What good has been done you!" Yochanan thundered. "You have been brought under the wings of God."

Almost immediately thereafter, Resh Lakish became gravely ill. The Rabbis were convinced that he fell ill because he had offended the highly esteemed Rabbi Yochanan. Resh Lakish's wife, who was Rabbi Yochanan's sister, pleaded with her brother to pray for her husband's recovery, but he refused. "If not for my husband's sake," she implored, "then pray for the sake of my children, that they not become orphans."

"I will take care of your children if your husband dies," Rabbi Yochanan responded.

"Then pray for my sake," his sister pleaded. "Pray that I not become a widow."

"I will support you if your husband dies," was all her brother would say.

A short time later, Resh Lakish did die, and Rabbi Yochanan fell into a deep depression. The Rabbis sent Elazar ben Pedat, the brightest young scholar they could find, to study with him, hoping that the youthful sage's sharp mind would divert Rabbi Yochanan from his grief.

Rabbi Elazar ben Pedat sat before Rabbi Yochanan, and each time the older rabbi uttered an opinion, he would say, "I know another source that supports what you are saying."

Rabbi Yochanan finally said to him, "Do you suppose you are like Resh Lakish? Whenever I stated an opinion, Resh Lakish would raise twenty-four objections to what I said. . . . He forced me to justify every ruling I gave, so that in the end, the subject was fully clarified. But all you do is tell me that you know another source that supports what I am saying. Don't I know myself that what I have said is right?"

Rabbi Yochanan turned away from the young man, rent his garments, and staggered about weeping. "Where are you, son of Lakish?" he repeatedly cried out.

In the end, he lost his reason. The Rabbis prayed that God would take mercy on him, and soon thereafter he died.[1]

The quarrel between Rabbi Yochanan and Resh Lakish is surely one of the Talmud's saddest stories.[2] Two men who are best friends have a falling-out, and one dies before they can make peace. The survivor is so inconsolable that the only peace that can assuage his pain is death. Perhaps the most poignant aspect of the story is the relatively minor nature of the dispute that yielded such tragedy.

This tale's most important lesson applies to everyone: No matter how angry you become during an argument, always remain focused on the issue at hand. *Never use damaging personal information to invalidate your adversary's contentions.* You must remain fair and measured in your words, even when you're upset.

I remember reading years ago that the renowned actress Lynn Fontanne, when asked for the secret of her successful marriage to, and acting partnership with, Alfred Lunt, an equally renowned actor, she responded that they were never uncivil to one another. Respect and civility are the preconditions for a fair fight. This means internalizing the talmudic admonition to "let your friend's honor be as dear to you as your own"—even, or especially, when you're having a dispute.[3]

An inability to follow this simple rule is what transforms so many relatively moderate arguments into angry quarrels that lead to ruptures between friends and close family members.

For many years, during lectures, I have asked audiences: "In how many of your families are there relatives who no longer are on speaking terms?" Almost invariably, a third of those present, or even a little more, raise their hands.

When I ask people to describe the origins of these family feuds, they usually report quarrels that began over minor matters and then escalated. What caused this escalation? The very intimacy of the relationship provided the adversaries with destructive information that they could use against each other and also ensured that their harsh words would have an impact.

This is a common pattern in quarrels that rip families apart and destroy friendships. In one family I know, the fight between a brother and a sister began over their father's obituary notice. The local newspaper had reported that the deceased was living in his oldest son's house at the time of his death. Although true, this announcement infuriated the daughter, with whom the father had resided for many years before moving into his son's house. She was irate that her brother had not made sure to have this fact included in the obituary.

Within days of the father's death, every act of her brother that she had disapproved of was raised, dissected, and condemned during increasingly acrimonious exchanges. I suspect that the brother was soon responding with some angry recollections and charges of his own. Although this fight occurred more than fifteen years ago, the siblings have had only the most superficial contact since. Of one thing I am certain: the aged father, whose obituary notice had set off this dispute, would have been brokenhearted.

"Hatred makes a straight line crooked," an ancient Hebrew proverb teaches. When people become angry, their reason becomes "bent." Suddenly, someone who is ordinarily quite kind and responsible, such as Rabbi Yochanan, can say terrible things. Because he did not have a compelling argument with which to defeat Resh Lakish, Rabbi Yochanan employed a highly personal one: How could anyone prefer Resh Lakish's reasoning to his, given that the former had been a gladiator and thief?

When Resh Lakish did not back off from his challenge and, indeed, counterattacked Yochanan for humiliating him, the latter grew even angrier. An hour before their dispute, had you asked Rabbi Yochanan to name his greatest disciple and closest friend, he undoubtedly would have answered, "Resh Lakish." Yet after exchanging a few harsh words, even the prospect of Resh Lakish's death did not soften his attitude. "I'll take care of your orphaned children," he assured his sister. "I'll support you if you become a widow."

How irrelevant those guarantees were! She hadn't come to her brother because she was worried about financial support for her family; rather, she wanted the two most important men in her life, her husband and her brother, to make peace. She must have been thinking: *If Yochanan goes to visit my husband even now, perhaps he can still recover.* But because Rabbi Yochanan would not "unharden" his heart, both men were ultimately doomed.

Every year, tens of thousands of families are split asunder, and close friendships are broken, because contending parties refuse to fight fairly. In a dispute with someone, you have the right to state your case, express your opinion, explain why you think the other party is wrong, even make clear how passionately you feel about the matter at hand. *But these are the only rights you have.* You do not have a moral right to undercut your adversary's position by invalidating him or her personally. It is unethical to dredge up past information about the person—information with which you're most likely familiar because of your formerly close association—and use it against him or her.

Yet people do so routinely, then become furious when the other person breaks off contact or fights back with similar arguments. Words have consequences, and if you use them to hurt people, your victims will find ways to hurt you in return. This is what happened between Rabbi Yochanan and Resh Lakish. The way to avoid such bitterness in your life is to learn how to fight—fairly.

CHAPTER 8

How to Criticize and How to Accept Rebuke

Whoever can stop the members of his household from committing a sin, but does not, is held responsible for the sins of his household. If he can stop the people of his city from sinning, but does not, he is held responsible for the sins of the people of his city. If he can stop the whole world from sinning, and does not, he is held responsible for the sins of the whole world.

—Babylonian Talmud, *Shabbat* 54b

Be not angry that you cannot make others as you wish them to be since you cannot make yourself as you wish to be.

—Thomas à Kempis

THE PROPHET NATHAN provides a biblical model of how to reprove someone effectively. When he learns that King David has committed adultery with Bathsheba and arranged for her husband, Uriah, to die in battle, the prophet realizes that he must confront the king. He does so in private, intent on moving David to recognize the great evil that he has committed.

Nathan comes before the king and tells him of a minor but disturbing injustice that has recently been brought to his attention:

> *There were two men in the same city, one rich and one poor. The rich man had very large flocks and herds, but the poor man had only one little ewe lamb that he had bought. He tended it and it grew up together with him and his children; it used to share his morsel of bread, drink from his cup, and nestle in his bosom. . . . One day, a traveler came to the rich man, but he was loath to take anything from his own flocks or herds to prepare a meal for the guest who had come to him; so he took the poor man's lamb [slaughtered it] and prepared it for the man who had come to him.*
>
> *David flew into a rage against the man, and said to Nathan, "As the Lord lives, the man who did this deserves to die! . . ."*
>
> *And Nathan said to David, "That man is you!"* (II Samuel 12:1–7)

Nathan knows that he has the moral responsibility to confront King David about his very serious offenses, but he also recognizes the necessity of presenting his reproof in a way that will be effective and thereby force David to acknowledge his wrongdoing. Had he confronted David "directly," labeling him an adulterer and also a killer, the king would probably have reacted defensively, as most of us do when caught doing something wrong. He might well have come up with a long list of excuses, perhaps something like: "I didn't intend to commit adultery, I was just overcome with passion. When Bathsheba told me she was pregnant, the last thing in the world I wanted was to have Uriah killed. I summoned him from the battlefield, then urged him to go home and spend the night with his wife. That way, Uriah would have assumed the baby was his. But he refused. I even ordered him to go home—twice—and both times he disobeyed me. So he left me no choice. Had I done nothing, then he would have come back later and found Bathsheba pregnant with a child not his, and would have harmed her. Besides, what if it became known that I had lain with one of my officers' wives while they were off fighting for me? It might have caused them to mutiny. I am the king of Israel; the country's entire destiny rests on my shoulders. For the country's survival, it was my duty to have Uriah killed."

Instead, by depersonalizing his critique, Nathan enables the king to see the issue's moral simplicity: he has taken another man's wife, just as the rich man stole the lamb that the poor man loved. Once David has pronounced his verdict on the fictitious rich man, "The man who did this deserves to die!" and Nathan responds, "That man is you!" the king has no choice but to acknowledge that he deserves the same withering condemnation. David finally understands that all the tortured rationales in the world cannot wipe away his act of adultery and Uriah's innocent blood.

Thus, because Nathan knows how to offer criticism, David learns how to repent.

Fortunately, few of us will ever have to rebuke another person for such monumental offenses. However, in our closest relationships, we often have reason, and even the obligation, to offer criticism, whether it is to express justified anger (see chapter 6), to protect innocent people from being harmed, or to benefit some other person. Indeed, the Torah includes criticizing those who have done wrong among its 613 commandments: "Reprove your kinsman, but incur no guilt because of him" (Leviticus 19:17).

Scholars generally interpret the commandment's last words, "but incur no guilt because of him," as obliging you to speak up lest you share in the responsibility for another's destructive behavior. For example, if a friend is drunk and about to drive a car, this commandment obligates you to do everything possible to stop him from doing so. If you don't make a serious effort to stop him, you share in the guilt for any injuries he may cause.

This commandment also enjoins us to offer rebuke in all instances in which we think we can help minimize harmful behavior. Perhaps you have a friend who verbally attacks his spouse or tries to "improve" his child's behavior in a manner that humiliates the young person. Speaking up in such a situation usually is quite uncomfortable, but remaining silent is grossly irresponsible and helps ensure that the harmful behavior continues.

A second interpretation of "incur no guilt because of him" has been proposed by several thinkers: although you're permitted, and sometimes obligated, to reprove another, it is sinful to do so in a demeaning or humiliating way. If you criticize someone in order to stop her from committing a serious misdeed, running the risk of embarrassing her might not seem so terrible (although the humiliation she feels will make it less likely that your words will affect her behavior). On the other hand, if you're reproving someone about a less significant matter (for instance, a child who has irresponsibly broken something), you're never justified in shaming that person. If you do, trying to eliminate a minor wrong will have caused you to commit a major one. Instead, your goal should be to find a way of criticizing that inflicts the minimum of hurt while doing the maximum of good.

Consider the following recollection of the late Isaac Asimov, the author and editor of more than 500 books (along with an estimated 90,000 letters and postcards), who is regarded by numerous admirers as one of America's premier intellects. Asimov himself was forthright about his high self-estimation: "I have always thought of myself as a remarkable fellow, even from childhood, and I have never wavered in that opinion."[1]

If ever there was a person whose ego might have been impervious to tactless criticism, it would seem to be Asimov. Yet in his posthumously published memoirs, he recounts an incident that he could never forget.

As a fifteen-year-old high school student, Asimov had enrolled in a writing class taught by a man named Max N. The teacher's first assignment was to have the students write an essay. When he asked for volunteers to read their efforts before the class, Asimov raised his hand. "I had read only about a quarter of it," he recalls in his memoirs, "when N. stopped me and used an opprobrious barnyard term to describe my writing. I had never heard a teacher use a 'dirty word' before and I was shocked. The class wasn't however. They laughed at me very uproariously and I took my seat in bitter shame."[2]

Although hurt and humiliated, Asimov conceded then, and in his memoirs, that N.'s negative assessment of his writing was correct. He had attempted an affected literary style; what emerged was "absolutely, terminally rotten." So he took the teacher's negative reaction to heart and a few months later wrote a lighthearted piece that N. printed in the school's literary journal. It was the first significant Asimov piece ever published.

But when he thanked N. for running the piece, the teacher wounded him again, saying that he'd published it only because he needed a light piece to round out the issue and every other submission had a serious tone.

Seventy when he wrote his memoirs, Asimov knew that he was terminally ill (he died two years later, in 1992). Yet anyone who reads this account realizes how fresh his pain was, even after fifty-five years. "I hate very few people," Asimov writes of Max N., "but I hate *him*." He confides a long-standing fantasy: "I wish I had a time machine and could go back to 1934 with some of my books and some of the articles that have been written about me and say to him, 'How do you like that, you rotten louse? You didn't know whom you had in your class. If you had treated me right, I could have recorded you as my discoverer, instead of branding you a rotten louse.'"[3]

If even as self-assured a person as Isaac Asimov can be so devastated by harsh criticism—he describes this episode as "the hardest blow my ego has ever received"—consider how many less hardy souls we may have wounded through tactless and wounding words.[4]

To avoid being needlessly cruel, before you speak, ask yourself the following three questions:

1. How do I feel about offering this criticism? Does it give me pleasure or pain?

"Love unaccompanied by criticism is not love," an ancient Jewish text teaches.[5] Yet, as a general rule, criticism unaccompanied by love—or at least sincere concern—won't help the person being criticized. If you realize that part of you relishes speaking out, you probably shouldn't. The insincerity of your concern, your pleasure at seeing your victim's discomfort, or your desire to hurt someone with whom you might be angry will probably be apparent, and your listener will react defensively. Imagine yourself in the place of the person being criticized: If you sense that the speaker is enjoying his or her task, wouldn't that provoke anger and denial in you rather than self-examination?

If you really wish you didn't have to offer the criticism, but feel morally obligated to do so, the purity of your motives will shine through in the encounter. It's likely that the listener won't see you as an adversary who wants to inflict hurt, but as a friend who wants to help, a perception that will enable him to maintain self-respect and self-esteem ("He's criticizing me because he likes me and thinks that if I just correct this trait, everything will be all right").[6]

Before you criticize anyone, think about this directive given to medical students: "Your first obligation is to do no harm." Unless you're confident that both the content and tone of your words will help the listener to overcome a specific flaw rather than demoralize him or her, keep silent.

2. Does my criticism offer specific ways to change?

Because it's difficult to criticize someone in a manner that will induce change, Maimonides offered very specific tactical advice: "He who rebukes another, whether for offenses against the rebuker himself or for sins against God, should administer the rebuke in private, speak to the offender gently and tenderly, and point out that he is only speaking for the wrongdoer's own good."[7]

Contrast Maimonides's counsel with the behavior of Asimov's writing teacher. Maimonides advises the person who is offering the criticism to do so in private; the first time N. criticized Asimov, he did so before the whole class. Maimonides advises that one should offer the criticism "gently and tenderly"; N. spoke brutally to Asimov, both publicly and privately. Maimonides advises us to point out that we are offering criticism only for the listener's good. Yet, when N. criticized Asimov, he clearly wasn't doing so for Asimov's sake.[8]

Imagine how a writing teacher who had compassion for Asimov might have responded. Rather than dismissing the young student with a vulgar word, he would probably have kept him after class and shown him how artificial his writing style sounded. Even if the teacher felt the need to offer a public critique in order to teach the rest of the class, he could have done so without making the young student feel like so abject a failure. Is it not obvious that a teacher who liked Asimov, or at least felt some sympathy for him, would have searched for a gentler way to offer his criticism? For example, N. could have selected several sentences that did not work and demonstrated how they weakened Asimov's writing. Instead, N. spoke harshly because he wanted his words to hurt; he was precisely the sort of person who should not offer criticism.

3. Are my words nonthreatening and reassuring?

It is told of the nineteenth-century Jewish moralist Rabbi Israel Salanter that when he offered criticisms during public lectures, he would announce: "Don't think that I am innocent of all the offenses I am enumerating. I too have committed some of them. All that I am doing, therefore, is speaking aloud to myself, and if anything you might overhear applies to you also, well and good."

Salanter's technique can be very effective in making criticism sound nonthreatening and encouraging. If you yourself have grappled with the trait you're criticizing, be sure to say so. If you're not guilty of the fault, you can cite your own struggles with comparable faults and the efforts you have made to overcome them. Acknowledging your weaknesses shows your listener that you are not setting yourself above him or her. And describing your attempts to change may offer the person the inspiration or some strategies to do the same.

If you want someone to be open to your criticism, avoid making blanket statements that demoralize him. Confine your remarks to specific incidents. Critics who use words such as "always" or "never" ("You're *always* thinking only about what's good for you. You don't consider anybody else's needs," or "You *never* think before you act") in effect compel their listener to react defensively. What person, the critic included, would be willing to acknowledge, in the face of such criticism, that she only cares about what's good for herself or would say, "I am really stupid. I never think before I act." And when directed against a child, words such as "always" and "never" can permanently distort the child's self-image.

In addition to being psychologically damaging, extreme accusations are unethical because they are almost always untrue. You yourself know that it is not true that your listener "*never* thinks before" he acts. You might think that you occupy the moral high ground relative to the person you are criticizing, but if you lie or grossly exaggerate his faults, you have done something wrong and you lose the moral high ground that you think entitles you to offer the criticism in the first place.

We tend to use unconditional words when we are angry, a time when it is hard for almost everyone not to exaggerate and otherwise distort the truth. If you find that you do so often, recall these wise words of Simcha Zissel Ziv, a nineteenth-century Eastern European rabbinic sage (his advice was offered in the context of a classroom setting but has far broader applicability): "Very often a teacher will become angry at a student who is rebuked three or four times and still does not listen. Before losing patience, the teacher should ask himself if he always corrects his own shortcomings by the third or fourth reminder."[9]

Sometimes criticism is most eloquent when not expressed in words. Take the nineteenth-century Hasidic Rabbi Israel of Vishnitz, who wished to influence the behavior of a certain banker. He was well aware that a frontal critique, even if accompanied by words of affection, almost certainly would backfire. Guided by the talmudic admonition "Just as one is commanded to say that which will be heeded, so is one commanded *not* to say that which will *not* be heeded," the rabbi used a different approach:[10]

"Rabbi Israel of Vishnitz was in the habit of strolling with his assistant (*gabbai*) for a half hour every evening. On one such occasion, they stopped in front of the house of a certain wealthy bank manager. The man was known to be a *maskil*, a follower of the 'Enlightenment' movement, i.e., anything but a follower of the rebbe [the Hasidic term for a rabbinic leader]. Rabbi Israel knocked on the door and, when a servant opened it, entered the house. The puzzled assistant, without asking a word, followed the rebbe inside.

"The bank manager received his distinguished guest respectfully and politely. The rebbe took the seat that was offered him, and sat for quite some time without saying a word. Knowing that protocol would deem it impertinent to ask the rebbe directly the reason for his visit, the host whispered his question to the rebbe's assistant, who shrugged his shoulders. After a good while, the rebbe rose to leave, and bid his host farewell. The bank manager accompanied him to the door and, his understandable curiosity getting the better of him, asked: 'Could you please explain to me, rebbe, why you honored me with a visit?'

"'I went to your house in order to fulfill a *mitzvah* [religious commandment],' the rebbe replied, 'and thank God I was able to fulfill it.'

"'And which *mitzvah* was that?' asked the confused bank manager.

"'Our Sages teach that "Just as one is commanded to say that which will be listened to, so is one commanded not to say that which will not be listened to." Now if I remain in my house and you remain in yours, what kind of mitzvah is it that I refrain from telling you "that which will not be listened to"? In order to fulfill the *mitzvah* properly, one obviously has to go to the house of the person who will not listen, and *there* refrain from speaking to him. And that is exactly what I did.'

"'Perhaps, rebbe,' said the bank manager, 'you would be so good as to tell me what this thing is. Who knows, perhaps I *will* listen?'

"'I am afraid you won't,' said the rebbe.

"The longer the rebbe refused, the greater grew the curiosity of the other to know the secret: he continued to press the rebbe to reveal 'that which would not be listened to.'

"'Very well,' said the rebbe finally. 'A certain penniless widow owes your bank quite a sum for the mortgage of her house. Within a few days, your bank is going to dispose of her house by public sale, and she will be out on the street. I had wanted to ask you to over-look her debt, but didn't, because of the *mitzvah* of "not saying . . ."'

"'But what do you expect me to do?' asked the bank manager in amazement. 'Surely you realize that the debt is not owed to me personally, but to the bank, and I am only its manager, and not its owner, and the debt runs into several hundreds, and if . . .'

"'It's exactly as I said all along,' the rebbe interrupted, 'that you would not want to hear.'

"With that he ended the conversation and walked away. The bank manager went into his house, but the rebbe's words found their way into his heart and gave him no rest until he paid the widow's debt out of his own pocket."[11]

Knowing how to offer criticism and effect change even when you are not directly criticizing—*that* is a trait we should all strive to acquire.

AS CHALLENGING AS it is to criticize properly, it is even harder to accept rebuke. When criticized, many of us deny or minimize the faults being pointed out; we blame somebody else, perhaps even the critic; or we insist, both to the person offering the criticism and ourselves, that we cannot change. Even as the critic speaks, we are already formulating a counterattack.

According to the Bible, this problem is as old as humankind. When God rebukes Adam for eating from the tree of "the knowledge of good and evil," an act that God had specifically forbidden, Adam blames Eve. "The woman You put at my side—she gave me of the tree and I ate" (Genesis 3:12). In fact, the implication of Adam's words is that not just Eve but God too is responsible, since it was He Who put her at Adam's side. When God confronts Eve over the sin, she blames the snake. "The serpent duped me, and I ate" (Genesis 3:13). Note that Eve skirts the fact that she then encouraged Adam to do so as well.

Some years later, when God calls out to Cain immediately after he has murdered his brother, "Where is your brother Abel?" the killer responds, "I do not know. Am I my brother's keeper?" (Genesis 4:9).

It would appear that the passing of centuries did not encourage people to be more open to criticism. The second-century talmudic scholar Rabbi Tarfon lamented: "I wonder if there is anyone in this generation who knows how to accept criticism, for if one says to another, 'Remove the chip of wood from between your eyes,' the other answers, 'Remove the beam from between *your* eyes.'"[12]

Of course, there are some cases when counter-criticizing—or better yet, ignoring—the messenger is appropriate. If someone is constantly noting things you are doing wrong and rarely tells you when you've done something right, there's a good chance the person doesn't like you or that these criticisms are overstated and unfair. In addition, the critic who makes you feel that your problem is immense and uncorrectable is not offering constructive advice. To criticize a person for an uncorrectable fault makes as much sense as a woman saying to a man, "I could really love you—if you were only an inch and a half taller." Such needlessly hurtful words serve no one's interests.

On the other hand, if two people who are in a relationship—be it friendship or romantic—*never* criticize each other, neither grows morally. Chief Rabbi Abraham Isaac Kook of Israel was asked why he so loved the saintly Jerusalem scholar and teacher Rabbi Aryeh Levine. He responded: "For twenty years he has been frequenting my home and in all that time he has never flattered me. . . . If he ever saw me do anything which he did not understand, he questioned it or commented on it."[13]

Rabbi Kook's observation is particularly important for wealthy or powerful people, many of whom are surrounded by those who are too much in awe of them, or too frightened by them, to offer criticism. We all need people we can trust to question and criticize us when we act wrongly.

Do you have at least one friend (it could be your spouse) who speaks honestly to you and who criticizes you? If not, then you have no real friend.

MOST OF US, if we are honest about it, can tell the difference between unproductive rebukes and well-intentioned ones. Yet even loving criticism can be a bitter pill—perhaps because, being offered by the people who know us best, it's likely to highlight our true faults.

Many people, when criticized, fight back by saying something like, "So you think I have a bad temper? At least it hasn't alienated my children from me the way yours are alienated from you," or "You think I treated you unfairly in that deal? Well, it so happens that my reputation for honesty is higher than yours. If you think I am exaggerating, maybe we should ask some other people what they think."

Whenever you're tempted to employ so intemperate an argument, keep in mind that even if your critic possesses the flaws of which you accuse him, *so what?* If what he says about you is true, the fact that he himself has numerous flaws is *irrelevant*.

A friend of mine hosts a radio talk show. Although he passionately espouses often controversial political views, he makes it a point never to insult callers who dispute his positions. Rather, he listens carefully to what they say and responds vigorously but courteously. He told me that he reads emails from his listeners, *particularly* those written by people who clearly oppose—and sometimes abhor—his views. "I am anxious to read what they say," he explained to me. "Maybe I did say something unfair or wrong. The fact that I might disagree with these people on so many other issues doesn't mean that every criticism they make of me is wrong."

My friend's unusually open attitude toward others' criticism has been an acquired trait. In his early days as a public speaker, he often fended off his critics with sarcasm, biting wit, and occasional anger. He now says, "A person can't grow that way. You grow by hearing what your critics are saying and learning to distinguish what's true from what's false. You certainly don't grow if you only listen to people who just offer you praise."

Even more than being commendable, my friend's attitude offers a good lesson. Of course, it's likely that the person criticizing you has numerous faults; indeed, she even might be guilty of the very flaw that she is pointing out in you. But unless you have reason to believe that her real goal is to undermine your sense of self-worth, you should quash such thoughts as *What gives her the right to criticize me? Look at her flaws.* Instead, you should ask: *Is what she is saying true?* Even if the critic's point is exaggerated, that is no excuse to reject everything she has said. Instead, you should ask: *Is there some validity in the criticism? Can I take what she has said, and use it to improve myself?*

Only someone who is already perfect doesn't need to learn how to accept criticism, but such a person does not exist.

For people blessed with relatively thick skins, learning to accept criticism might not be difficult. (I'm speaking of those who take seriously what their critics say, not those who shrug off and ignore all critical comments.) More sensitive people may find it very difficult to listen carefully to critical words and not respond with anger, depression, or even tears. According to Jewish tradition, if a person is known to reject all criticism, or to respond to it with great anger, you're under no obligation to proffer it. If you are the kind of sensitive person to whom this applies, you might regard this ruling as a dispensation. However, it's hardly desirable. Having people conclude that you can't change your bad traits and that it's a waste of time to try to help you do so is hardly a great honor.

If you find it very difficult to accept criticism, try this experiment: The next few times you are being criticized, consciously try to change only one thing—your attitude toward the critic. Instead of reacting as if he or she is your adversary, remember this two-century-old challenge offered by the great Hasidic rebbe Rabbi Nachman of Bratslav: "If you are not going to be better tomorrow than you were today, then what need do you have for tomorrow?"

Indeed, what purpose is there to life if we can no longer grow, change, and improve? Animals live cyclically; for them, each day is the same as the preceding one, at least in terms of their personality traits. But human beings can grow, both through self-analysis and self-criticism and through the insights, encouragement, and criticisms of others.

Criticism, with its underlying assumption that we are still capable of change, should stimulate us; it implies that our souls, not just our bodies, are very much alive. Thus, we should regard someone who points out our correctable faults with the gratitude we feel toward a doctor who diagnoses an ailment. This very comparison occurred to one of Rabbi Salanter's disciples, the previously mentioned Rabbi Simcha Zissel Ziv: "A person is willing to pay a doctor for trying to heal him; should he be any less grateful to one who helps him correct his spiritual failings?"

Such corrections should go on for the entirety of your life. I know of people who have achieved reconciliations and spiritual growth on their deathbeds.

Rabbi Salanter used to recall an insight he had while spending an evening in the home of a shoemaker. Late at night, the man was feverishly working by the light of a candle whose flame was near extinction. "Why are you still working?" Rabbi Salanter asked him. "Look how late it is; your candle is about to go out."

"It is late," the shoemaker agreed. "But as long as the candle is burning, it is still possible to mend."[14]

CHAPTER 9

Between Parents and Children

A torn jacket is soon mended, but hard words bruise the heart of a child.

—Henry Wadsworth Longfellow

SOME 1,800 YEARS ago, a certain Rabbi Elazar was taking a leisurely ride alongside a lake on a donkey and feeling very proud of his considerable scholarly achievements.

Suddenly, the Talmud informs us, "he chanced upon an exceedingly ugly man, who greeted him, 'Peace be upon you, my master.'"

The man's disagreeable appearance shattered the rabbi's good cheer; instead of returning the greeting, he responded: "You worthless creature! How ugly you are! Are all the people of your city as ugly as you?"

"The man replied: 'What can I do about it? Go tell the Craftsman Who made me, "How ugly is the vessel You have made."'"

"Rabbi Elazar [immediately] realized that he had done wrong. He got down from the donkey and, prostrating himself before the man, said to him: 'I apologize to you; please forgive me!'"

"The man replied: 'I will not forgive you until you go to the Craftsman Who made me and tell Him: "How ugly is the vessel You have made."'"[1]

When I first came across this tale as a young rabbinical student in my early twenties, I was sure that it could never have happened, or that it was, at the least, grossly exaggerated, and believed that it was a fiction created by the Rabbis to teach a moral lesson. How could anyone, never mind an esteemed rabbi, be so cruel as to mock another person's bad looks? True, the Talmud depicts Rabbi Elazar as repenting, but how could he have said such a thing in the first place?

Since then, I have learned more from life than from books. The notion that, in just a moment, whether of self-satisfaction or great annoyance, a person of considerable stature could say something vicious no longer shocks me. In the intervening years, I have heard stories from friends and acquaintances and read memoirs of those who suffered equally cruel insults, and not from strangers, but from *parents*, the very people who claimed to love them more than any-one else.

Unquestionably, children's behavior can be frustrating and some-times enraging. It is easy for an overworked, anxiety-ridden parent to focus—and sometimes exclusively focus—on a child's incon-siderate, disobedient, or disrespectful actions. If you find yourself doing this, in addition to inflicting emotional harm on the child, you also are violating the important ethical norm of *ha-karat ha-tov*, "recognition of the good [another has done you]." For while the tantrums and self-absorption of young children can truly be infuriating or unnerving, it is not reasonable to judge them by adult behavioral standards. You should also realize that acts of disobedi-ence rarely tell the whole story.

My friend Terry Wohlberg, a Los Angeles–based psychothera-pist, notes that in the face of a tantrum or other difficult behavior, we might consider what could have caused our child to act in such a way. What needs, desires, or feelings are motivating her behavior? Did she have a hard day at school, or difficulty with a friend or in a class? Is she overtired and not feeling well? If we ask ourselves these or similar questions, we become more compassionate and kinder with our words. By talking with our children, we help them understand what is motivating their own behavior, and we also help them organize and make sense of their internal experience. Does this mean that we don't discipline? No, of course not. But as we verbally acknowledge the needs behind their behavior, we can help ensure that our reactions are communicated from a place of understanding and love, while we also still hold the line.

As the child psychologist Miriam Adahan wisely advises: "Remind yourself that your child performs thousands of acts of self-discipline . . . which you do not notice. There are thousands of times when he did come when you called, did eat the food he may not have wanted because you wanted him to, did give up some pleasurable activity to do your bidding even though it was painful for him at the time, did not bother you when you were busy, and did not fight or argue with you or his siblings."[2]

"Of course," you may think. How many parents have ever looked into the face of their sleeping child and wanted to do anything but help, protect, and cherish him or her? Yet no honest parent can say that he or she has never had an outburst of unchecked anger or never made a demeaning or insensitive remark to a child. What's more, many of us carry at least a few scars inflicted by words from our own parents:

A woman, highly self-conscious about being flat-chested throughout her teen years, still quails at the memory of her father's teasing: "When are you going to grow breasts and be a real woman?"

An accomplished lawyer, who as a young boy used to create minor disturbances in school, still chafes at his father's unkind threat: "Don't assume that we love you. In this household, you have to earn our love."

Eleanor Roosevelt never forgot how her mother would speak lovingly to her younger brothers, but not to her. "If a visitor was there," the First Lady confided to friends, "she might turn and say, 'She is such a funny child, so old-fashioned, we always call her Granny.' I wanted to sink through the floor in shame."[3]

A woman I know recalls being told by her mother: "Don't smile or laugh when you're in public. Your buck-teeth stick out, and you look terrible." To this day, whenever she laughs—and you can be sure that she almost always tries to suppress the impulse—this woman still covers her mouth with her hand.

Some of these examples of hurtful words said by parents may sound extreme, and it's not hard to recognize the tremendous power they have to wreak psychological damage. The enormous attention focused in recent years on the physical and sexual abuse of children is deserved, but fortunately children who suffer such abuse are still a definite minority. However, the victims of deeply hurtful and perhaps oft-repeated comments are far more numerous. Yet because this form of parental cruelty is rarely viewed as the serious matter it is, it's less frequently discussed. This is unfortunate, since the victims often carry its scars to their graves.

In the Jewish tradition, the prohibition against publicly shaming others applies as strongly to children as to adults.[4] In a world in which there is reason to believe that little attention was paid to children's emotional needs, the twelfth-century Jewish philosopher Moses Maimonides ruled: "Do not humiliate your fellow in public, whether he [or she] is a minor or an adult."5 Indeed, children are more vulnerable to all attacks, including humiliation. Therefore, if parents need to admonish a child, they should do so in private, just as they would with an adult. Parents who are quick-tempered must be especially careful not to violate this prohibition—for example, by berating a child in public or in the presence of his peers.

Unfortunately, many parents routinely violate this ethical norm. Some even humiliate their children for behavior that is beyond their control, such as learning disabilities or other disorders. A middle-aged man in his fifties recalled his shame and rage when he was six years old and still a bed-wetter, and his father said to him in front of the whole family: "We can't go on vacation and stay in a motel or at friends' homes because you still wet the bed. You are ruining the summer for all of us!" Dr. Abraham Twerski, a psychiatrist who knew the man, commented: "This was a totally unfair rebuke, because he was unable to control his bed-wetting, and [the man] said that his father's vicious criticism drove a stake into his heart. What was even worse was that this was said in the presence of his siblings. Thoughtless remarks such as this can have untold impact on a child, with long-term residuals of acrimony."6

I am not suggesting that parents must speak only kind and supportive words to their children, even when they act badly. They definitely have an obligation to teach their children right from wrong and to correct them when they misbehave. In Hebrew the word for parent (*horeh*) comes from the same root as that for teacher (*moreh*), an etymological suggestion that the parents' primary role is to teach. Indeed, parents who don't know *how* to teach, and *when* to speak up and correct, run the risk of raising unethical children who will turn into unethical adults.

The book of Samuel tells the story of Adonijah, son of King David, who, during the last year of his father's life, goes around Jerusalem boasting that soon he will be king. What was the root of his callous arrogance and disrespect toward his still living and reigning father? According to the Bible, David bore some of the blame because, throughout his son's life, "his father had never scolded him [and said], 'Why did you do that?'" (I Kings 1:5–6).

The biblical choice of words here is significant. The text doesn't say that David's error lay in not denouncing Adonijah for his poor character and selfish nature. So all-encompassing an attack probably would have been demoralizing and thus counterproductive. Rather, David's error, the Bible suggests, was in not criticizing Adonijah's bad acts as they occurred, in never asking him, "Why did you do that?"

By restricting criticism to a specific bad act, a parent is unlikely to damage a child's self-image.

Admittedly, finding the golden mean between being critical but not overly uncritical is difficult, but the alternative choice of many parents—vacillating between broad and destructive deprecatory comments and tolerating behavior that shouldn't be tolerated—is far worse.

Several years ago, close friends found that they were constantly criticizing their ten-year-old daughter for:

• Perpetually leaving her clothes strewn around her room

• Grabbing food with her hands straight off the plate and seldom using her fork

• Demanding things without saying "please" or responding "thank you" when she received them

• Not looking at people when they spoke to her

• Constantly breaking into her parents' conversations, even when they were on the phone

One night her father realized that from the time his daughter came home from school until she fell asleep, he and his wife were subjecting her to one long litany of complaints. He thought about how he would have felt had every aspect of his work and personality been criticized this way by his employer. Would his behavior really have improved or would he have lost all faith in his own competence? Would he have believed that his boss's constant rebukes were motivated by a loving desire for him to improve himself? Or would he have concluded that his boss probably didn't like him very much, and had a low opinion of his capabilities?

The following day the couple decided that instead of trying to turn their daughter into a perfect ten-year-old, they would focus their efforts for the time being on the one area about which they cared most: the child's moral character. From then on, politeness and gratitude, saying "please" and "thank you," became their one non-negotiable demand of her. They realized that unless their daughter's behavior improved in that area, she would grow up to be an unpleasant, unkind, and ultimately intolerable person. However, if she ended up a sloppy and even disorganized person, that would be unfortunate, but better that than feeling rejected by her own parents. (Also, there would be time to work on those traits later.)

Through their behavioral transformation, the parents demonstrated that they had internalized Henry Wadsworth Longfellow's penetrating insight: "A torn jacket is soon mended, but hard words bruise the heart of a child."

Parents commonly err not only in criticizing harshly but also in forgetting to praise. (This applies, by the way, even if your children are well into middle age.) In *Signs of the Times*, the religious writer Gottfried von Kronenberger relates an incident about a young mother who confessed to her pastor: "My little boy often misbehaves, and I have to scold him. But one day he had been especially good. That night, after I tucked him in bed and started downstairs, I heard him crying. I found his head buried in the pillow. Between sobs he asked, 'Mommy, haven't I been a pretty good boy today?'

"That question went through me like a knife," the mother told her pastor. "I had been quick to correct him when wrong, but when he had behaved, I hadn't noticed. I had put him to bed without a word of praise."[7]

The parental formula favored by some parents of "heavy on the criticism and light on the praise" causes children to go through life feeling inadequate as human beings and unworthy of being loved. The psychologist Haim Ginott advises mothers and fathers: "If you want your children to improve, let them overhear the nice things you say about them to others."

This should be obvious, but not to some people. I know a woman who was raised by a verbally abusive mother whose constant criticism was vicious. It was only after the mother's death at an early age that the girl learned from her mother's friends that the mother would read aloud to them letters the girl had written from camp, beautifully expressed letters in which the mother clearly took pride—a pride which would have been immensely meaningful to her daughter had she had thought to express it.

Also be certain that your children are made aware of nice things others say about them. I once came across an autobiographical recollection of a great pianist who remembered one day, as a child, overhearing his piano teacher tell his mother, "The boy has golden hands." From that day, the pianist recalled, he regarded his own hands with a certain awe. No matter how difficult a challenge he confronted at the keyboard, he was undaunted; after all, he had "golden hands."

Closely related to the problem of parents being overly critical of their children is the tendency of some parents to verbally wound their children through comparisons:

"Your brother never spills things. He tries to be careful. Why don't you?"

"Your sister always says 'please' and 'thank you.' I wish you would be polite and considerate like her."

"Your brother and sister don't get into trouble in school. You're the only one who's always causing us aggravation."

These sorts of comparisons spring to the lips of many parents, yet I can think of few more obvious violations of the Golden Rule. How many men would appreciate being told by their wives, "Mary's husband, Tom, also works long hours, but he doesn't complain every time she asks him to help around the house." And how many women would like to hear their bosses say, "If you could only learn to be more like Jill or Laura and be more innovative in your work"?

Throughout my childhood, until I went to college, I was a poor student. I tended to find schoolwork boring, and while I would read books about topics in which I was interested, I rarely did homework in those subjects in which I had no interest. My lackadaisical performance caused my parents considerable consternation. Two of my older cousins, who attended the same school, had graduated as valedictorians. My sister, also older than me, was very studious and ranked near the top of her class. On several occasions, our school's principal berated me (in front of the whole class no less): "What is the matter with you? You're a terrible student. I don't understand why you can't do even half as well as your cousins and sister. Your father's a scholar. Your grandfather's a scholar. What happened to you?" Needless to say, his words did not induce any improvement in my academic performance.

I remain, however, permanently grateful to my parents. Frustrated as they must have been by my mediocre school performance, and as often as they spoke to me about taking my schoolwork more seriously, I *never* recall them bringing my cousins and sister into the discussion. My parents intuitively understood that every criticism that can be directed toward a child can be made without reference to another sibling. I am also grateful to my grandfather, the rabbinical scholar to whom my principal referred, who one day said to the principal (and told me that he had said it), "You must not say such things to Joseph. One day he will become an important man and do great things, and you will regret your words."

Perhaps I haven't quite lived up to my grandfather's prophecy. Who could? But I know that what I have achieved in life is due in no small measure to the healing, supportive, and sometimes critical words of my parents and to my grandfather's absolute faith in me.

Comparisons with siblings are detrimental for another reason. Whether intended or not, such comparisons imply a parental preference for the other sibling. I often ask my audiences how many of them grew up feeling that one or both of their parents preferred one child over another. Many hands go up, and whenever those who felt less loved start to speak, deep expressions of pain gush forth. (I have also learned over the years that the favored children are frequently unhappy with their parents' favoritism. It often caused their siblings to resent them. Also, they frequently grew up feeling that their parents' happiness depended on their achievements.)

Parents have an obligation to ensure that all their children feel equally—or, perhaps better, as my friend Rabbi Irwin Kula suggests, "uniquely"—loved and appreciated. (Even if, in the privacy of their bedroom, they sometimes express a preference for one child over another, most parents know that such a preference is often temporary.) When they do not convey a feeling of love and appreciation, the damage they inflict is often lifelong. For with what greater disadvantage can a child go out into the world than with the feeling that even her own mother and father don't really love her?

In addition, comparing children undermines family unity. Instead of making the children feel that they are part of one united family ("one for all, and all for one"), children come to see themselves as competitors for a finite amount of parental love and approval. This type of competition rarely brings out the best in anyone, and it increases the likelihood that such children will not be close to each other when they grow up. As noted earlier, the Bible tells us that Jacob loved Joseph more than his other sons and made no effort to disguise his favoritism. He even had a special and exceedingly beautiful coat woven for Joseph. This and other acts of favoritism helped inflame Jacob's other sons against Joseph, and eventually they arranged to sell him as a slave into Egypt, while telling their father that a wild animal had killed him (Genesis 37). The Rabbis of the Talmud concluded from this episode that "a man should never single out one of his children for favorable treatment, for because of the two extra coins' worth of silk [woven into the special coat for Joseph] Joseph's brothers became jealous of him, and one thing led to another until our ancestors became slaves in Egypt."[8]

ON RAISING TRUTHFUL CHILDREN

Probably the most common reason children lie to their parents is that they are afraid of what might happen if they tell the truth. Two parents were exasperated by their five-year-old son's tendency to blame others, including ghosts, for mischievous things he did (such as writing with a crayon on the wall). They assured him that they would not get angry at him as long as he told the truth, but would be upset if he lied. After repeated reassurances from the parents, the boy started telling the truth consistently. Two years later, when the mother pressed him as to whether he had taken some important papers off her desk, he said, "Mommy, you know I don't lie anymore."

The German author Johann Paul Friedrich Richter wrote two centuries ago: "If a child tells a lie, tell him that he has told a lie, but don't call him a liar. If you define him as a liar, you break down his confidence in his own character."

My friend Dr. Isaac Herschkopf, a psychiatrist, has argued that far better even than telling a child he has lied is asking him questions in a Socratic style; once the conclusion is obvious, the child can rescind the lie and rectify it. When I asked Dr. Herschkopf how that works in real life, he told me of an incident when one of his daughters—who was, as he recalled, either three or four years old at the time—returned from nursery school with an expensive crayon set that he and his wife had not bought for her. When the parents asked where she got it, the girl answered, "I found it."

"Where did you find it?"

"In school."

"Where in school?"

"In an empty classroom."

"Why was the classroom empty?"

"Our class had left."

"Do you think someone might have left it behind?"

"Maybe."

"Any idea who?"

"I don't know."

"Did any of your classmates have that expensive crayon set?"

"Maybe."

"Who?"

"Dvora."

"Do you think therefore that Dvora left it behind?"

"Maybe."

"Maybe?"

"Probably."

"What do you think you should do?" (Note that they asked "What do you *think* you should do?" rather than "What do you *want* to do?")

"I should give it back to her."

"How will you explain not giving it back to her the same day?"

"I'll tell her the truth, that I took it home."

"By not telling her what to do," Dr. Herschkopf noted, "she could take full credit for returning the set, and by engaging in a Socratic dialogue, we, the parents, didn't have to back her into a corner and force her to lie, and we didn't have to point out her lies."

BETWEEN CHILDREN AND PARENTS

As regards the words children direct to parents, it is worth recalling that the Fifth of the Ten Commandments legislates: "*Honor* your father and mother." Although on three other occasions the Hebrew Bible commands love—of God (Deuteronomy 6:5), of one's neighbor (Leviticus 19:18), and of the stranger (Leviticus 19:34)—it does not command love of parents. In so intimate a relationship, it is hard to do so: either love is present or it isn't. What the Bible does demand is a measure of respect that can be expressed even during those painful periods when love might be lacking. It means that even when a child is furious at his parents, he doesn't cut them out of his life (except perhaps in those rare instances when a child has suffered physical, sexual, or serious emotional abuse at a parent's hands), and when she expresses anger, she avoids making comments like, "I hate you," or "I wish I had had decent parents, not you."

Many children grow up having been deeply hurt by their parents' words; by the time they become adolescents and adults, many have learned how to fight back—also with words. Usually, they are quite successful at hurting their parents in return, although the greater their success, the more pain they usually cause themselves. In his book *My Daddy Was a Pistol, and I'm a Son of a Gun*, the late Lewis Grizzard recalls going through his father's meager possessions at the hospital where he died. In the dead man's coat, Grizzard found a letter that he had evidently been carrying for a long time:

It was a letter from me. I had written it six months before. It was short, maybe a page, typewritten. Down at the end, I had given him some grief about straightening out his life. I told him I would have to think twice about inviting him to my house again if he didn't promise he wouldn't show up drinking. I'd just signed my name. I didn't say "love" or anything. I had just signed my name like I was a real hardass. I still wonder why he carried such a letter around with him for so long. Maybe he kept it as a reminder to do better. I don't know. Maybe he kept it to remind himself his only son was turning on him. Whatever, I never forgave myself for that letter. I can't get it out of my head he died not knowing how much I loved him.[9]

CHAPTER 10

The Cost of Public Humiliation

Whoever shames his neighbor in public, it is as if he shed his blood.

—Babylonian Talmud, *Bava Mezia* 58b

SOME 1,800 YEARS ago in Israel, Rabbi Judah the Prince, the leading scholar of his age, was delivering an important lecture when suddenly he found himself in a very aggravating circumstance: a member of the audience who had eaten a large amount of garlic was emitting such an unpleasant odor that the rabbi found it difficult to concentrate. Rabbi Judah abruptly stopped speaking and called out: "Whoever ate the garlic, leave!"

Almost immediately, Rabbi Hiyya, a scholar only slightly less prominent than the speaker, rose from his seat and started toward the back. Many other listeners, mortified by Rabbi Hiyya's public embarrassment, followed him out, and the lecture was canceled.

The next morning, Rabbi Judah's son confronted Rabbi Hiyya and criticized him for spoiling his father's lecture.

"God forbid that I would ever trouble your father," Rabbi Hiyya responded.

"How can you deny what you did?" the son answered. "Wasn't it you who stood up when my father demanded that the one who had eaten the garlic leave?"

"I stood up only to avoid the public humiliation of the person whose breath was bothering your father. Since I already have a certain status among the rabbis, I was willing to accept the embarrassment of being publicly singled out like that. Imagine, though, if the person who had eaten the garlic was a rabbi of lesser stature than me, or worse, a student. *That* person would have been deeply humiliated, and likely would have become an object of mockery."*

So far we have been examining the cost of harsh words spoken in anger or criticism. But what of the occasional cruelties to which we are all prone? In the preceding example, Rabbi Hiyya was concerned with more than just guarding the unfortunate garlic eater's dignity. He also wished to prevent Rabbi Judah from violating one of Judaism's most serious ethical offenses: humiliating a fellow human being.

"Whoever shames his neighbor in public," the Talmud teaches, "it is as if he shed his blood."[1] The analogy is deemed apt because a shamed person's skin blanches as the blood drains from his face. The analogy is apt for yet another reason: sometimes a person who feels extremely humiliated wishes he were dead. Public humiliation can and has led to suicide. In a case that received national attention in 2010, Tyler Clementi, a freshman at Rutgers University, jumped off the George Washington Bridge after he learned that his roommate set up a webcam to catch him in a homosexual encounter in the room they shared; the roommate then used social media to encourage others to watch Clementi's encounter.

Clementi's case is, of course, not a singular occurrence. Some years ago, *People* magazine reported on the suicide of an over-

---

* The Babylonian Talmud, *Sanhedrin* 11a, recounts this incident. I have greatly expanded on Rabbi Hiyya's terse explanation for his behavior, putting into his mouth statements that are only suggested in the text and commentaries.

weight teenage girl who had been mocked (I am not using the word "teased" because it does not adequately convey the maliciousness of mockery) with cruel nicknames and comments by her peers. The article prompted this letter: "As a teenager, I too was tortured by my fellow students. I was an overweight teen and was abused constantly. I could not escape it. Teachers witnessed this over and over again and did nothing. The principal told me her hands were tied. I thought of suicide but luckily I never did it. . . . I wish all teenagers who tease others could have it happen to them so they could feel the pain and humiliation they inflict. I am signing this letter with the name they chose to torture me with for six years. How would you like to be known to an entire school as Big Bertha."

Not surprisingly, Jewish ethics—and I would hope all ethical systems—forbids calling someone by a nickname that hurts them (and people have the right to determine which nicknames hurt them). Teaching this to children is particularly important, since they often inflict cruel nicknames on their peers.[2]

Even when they note the terrible effects that public humiliation can have on its victims, not enough journalists, prominent figures, and opinion-makers—and for that matter, ordinary citizens—seem to feel abhorrence at the thought of shaming others.

In this chapter, I focus on both recent and not-so-recent events to indicate how long-standing a problem public humiliation is. In 1959, a prominent businessman donated half a million dollars to a university in Saint Louis, Missouri. The *St. Louis Post-Dispatch* assigned reporters to write a feature about him. The reporters soon discovered that the man had served three prison terms, totaling almost ten years, for forgery, larceny, and issuing fraudulent checks. In the thirty-five years since he had left prison, his record had been spotless; in fact, the FBI had cleared him for defense-related work. More significantly, there was no reason to believe that any of his current money, including the $500,000 he had donated to the university, had been earned illegally.

Nonetheless, the newspaper's headline on the article about him, which initially was supposed to be complimentary, described him as an "ex-convict." The man's wife and son, both of whom did not know of his earlier criminal record, denounced the piece as "vicious," to which the paper's managing editor responded: "I think the stories simply speak for themselves."[3]

The Talmud's moral standard differs markedly from that of the paper's managing editor. "If a person is a penitent," it teaches, "it is forbidden to say to him, 'Remember your early deeds.'"[4] Needless to say, it's even more cruel to spread embarrassing reports about a person *to others* when his or her subsequent behavior has been exemplary.

The newspaper's article was harmful to far more people than just this man and his family; it sent a very demoralizing message to everyone who has tried to redeem themselves after past misdeeds. It told them that no matter how hard they tried—whether through hard work, charitable contributions, or any form of "doing good"— they would forever be linked to the worst acts of their lives and could never win back their good name. Wouldn't this message alone make a person feel that there is little point in changing his ways?

The irony of the message communicated by the *St. Louis Post-Dispatch* "exposé" is profound: Years earlier, criminal courts had justifiably punished the man for doing evil. Now the newspaper was punishing him for doing good.

This case is unusual. As a rule, reporters and newspapers rarely go out of their way to humiliate someone against whom they have no grudge. More commonly, journalists, like many of us, are apt to shame only those with whom they already are angry.

The desire to humiliate adversaries is particularly common in politics. When South Carolinian Tom Turnipseed ran for Congress in 1980, his Republican rival unearthed and publicized evidence that Turnipseed had many years earlier suffered an episode of depression for which he had received electric shock treatment. When Turnipseed responded with an anguished attack on his opponent's campaign ethics, Lee Atwater (who later became famous as the director of George H. W. Bush's 1988 presidential campaign but was then directing the Republican campaign in South Carolina) responded that he had no intention of answering charges made by a person "hooked up to jumper cables."[5]

What a grotesque violation of privacy and the dictum against publicly humiliating another! Atwater put into the voters' heads a vicious, graphic image that potentially poisoned their perceptions not only of Turnipseed but also of everyone who had had electric shock therapy. As the *New York Times* reporter Eleanor Randolph noted twenty years later: "No matter how much Mr. Turnipseed talked about education or crime or dirty tricks after that, voters only saw the jumper cables."[6]

This story has a poignant postscript. Ten years later, Atwater himself was stricken with an inoperable brain tumor. Finding himself attached to unpleasant hospital machinery, and facing his own mortality, he was moved to write Turnipseed a letter asking forgiveness: "It is very important to me to let you know that out of everything that has happened in my career, one of the low points remains the so-called 'jumper-cable' episode." He then added, "My illness has taught me something about the notion of humanity, love, brotherhood, and relationships that I never understood, and probably never would have [if not for my illness]. So, from that standpoint, there is some truth and good in everything."[7]

In contemporary America, one of the most prestigious professions, the law, commonly encourages its practitioners to humiliate those who oppose them in court. Particularly among criminal defense lawyers, humiliating an opposing witness is sometimes regarded as a singularly effective way to discredit testimony. Seymour Wishman, a successful and well-known criminal defense attorney, recalls a difficult defense he had to mount for a client accused of raping and sodomizing a nurse.

Although Wishman had no reason to assume that the nurse had fabricated the allegation, he was very pleased when he learned that the examining police physician had neglected to mention in his medical report whether there was any physical evidence that force had been used against the nurse. This omission freed him to pursue a particularly aggressive cross-examination of the woman filled with reputation-damaging and humiliating questions:

WISHMAN: Isn't it a fact that after you met the defendant at a bar, you asked him if he wanted to have a good time?

WITNESS: No! That's a lie!

WISHMAN: Isn't it true that you took him and his three friends back to your apartment and had that good time?

WITNESS: No!

WISHMAN: And, after you had that good time, didn't you ask for money?

WITNESS: No such way!

WISHMAN: Isn't it a fact that the only reason you made a complaint was because you were furious for not getting paid?

WITNESS: No! No! That's a lie!

WISHMAN: You claim to have been raped and sodomized. As a nurse, you surely have an idea of the effect of such an assault on a woman's body. Are you aware . . . that the police doctors found no evidence of force or trauma?

WITNESS: I don't know what the doctors found.

After the trial ended, Wishman was proud when the presiding judge congratulated him for dealing with the woman "brilliantly." He felt considerably less proud half a year later when he happened to encounter the nurse at her workplace. As soon as she recognized Wishman, she started screaming: "That's the son-of-a-bitch that did it to me!"[8]

Of course, she was referring not to the alleged rape and sodomy, but to the verbal "rape" to which the lawyer had subjected her. According to Wishman, this encounter left him shaken and feeling somewhat guilty.

What is most amazing is the lawyer's surprise at his own reaction. Why shouldn't he have felt upset? It is difficult to imagine a greater cruelty toward, and humiliation of, a woman than to suggest that she was a prostitute who had made a false allegation of rape because she hadn't been paid.*

---

* The cruel behavior to which some lawyers will sink is well documented by Dominick Dunne in *Justice* (New York: Crown, 2001), 237–238. Dunne recounts the behavior of O. J. Simpson's lead defense lawyer in the wrongful death suit for the killing of Nicole Simpson and Ron Goldman. (Unlike the criminal trial, at which Simpson was found not guilty, at the civil trial for damages he was found guilty.) Goldman, from what can be deduced, died at the hands of O. J. Simpson trying to save Nicole and himself. Goldman, who had an emergency medical technician license and had done volunteer work with disabled children, dreamed of opening a restaurant, even though he was only twenty-five at the time of his death. The lawyer, hoping to hold down any possible jury award to Goldman's family, said: "Let's examine reality. Ron Goldman wouldn't have a restaurant now. He would be lucky to have a credit card." As Dunne commented: "The tone of [the lawyer's] voice matched the ugliness of his words." Elsewhere, Dunne noted: "To my way of thinking, one of the worst things a defense attorney can do is mock the dead victim his client is on trial for killing."

Atwater's and Wishman's very sincere regrets—and I recognize that it was courageous of them to make their earlier actions and their repentance widely known—bring to mind a striking image in the epilogue to George Bernard Shaw's play *Saint Joan*. The scene is set some twenty-five years after Joan of Arc has been convicted of heresy and burned at the stake. When a group of people gather to discuss her impact on their lives, one man says that he feels fortunate to have been present at her execution, because having seen how dreadful it was to burn a person, he subsequently became much kinder. "Must then a Christ perish in torment in every age," another character asks, "for the sake of those who have no imagination?"[9]

Is it just some journalists, politicians, and lawyers who lack the empathy to understand how wrong it is to humiliate others? Apparently many of us share in this failing, because thousands of individuals are shamed by others every day. The settings in which this emotional pain is inflicted may be less public, but the damage done can be just as devastating.

Take the case of a woman I know, Joanne, who is in her mid-thirties and a middle manager at a large corporation. Her job includes making public addresses and briefings, but for years her professional advancement has been stunted because of her inordinate fear of public speaking.

To Joanne and her many friends, her extreme nervousness has never made sense. Since she has considerable professional expertise and is very articulate about her work in one-on-one settings, they see no logical reason for her to freeze up every time she is called upon to make an address in public.

In desperation, Joanne consulted a psychologist, who hypnotized her. After inducing a deep state of relaxation, the psychologist instructed her to focus on any recollections or associations involving discomfort around public speaking. Joanne began to regress and was soon vividly reliving a series of episodes that had occurred when she was seven years old. At that time, her parents had recently moved from Argentina to Brazil. Although Joanne quickly acquired an adequate grasp of Portuguese, she still made many grammatical mistakes. Unfortunately, her second-grade teacher delighted in summoning Joanne to the blackboard at the front of the classroom and questioning her on material the class had been studying. On several occasions when she answered correctly but made grammatical mistakes, the teacher would ridicule her. After a few such episodes, Joanne chose not to answer at all. "Why do you stand there like a dummy?" the teacher would ask her. "Do you expect the answer to drop down to you from God in heaven?"

Twenty-five years later, this highly accomplished adult still finds herself paralyzed when called upon to speak in front of an audience. The schoolteacher's gratification of a sadistic impulse left Joanne with a lifelong emotional scar. To this day, she continues to go to great (and, from a career standpoint, self-destructive) lengths to avoid situations where she again might be humiliated.

Roberta, another woman I know, recalls a recurring and humiliating trauma from her teenage years. As a young child, she had been her mother's favorite. But when she became an adolescent and gained twenty pounds, her mother's expressions of love turned to withering verbal attacks.

Once, when her aunt was visiting, Roberta brought some food to the kitchen table. As she walked away, her mother said to her aunt in a loud voice: "Do you see how big her ass is, how fat she's become? Doesn't it look disgusting? People vomit when they see her." The mother repeated this sentiment many times, often in the presence of others.

During her high school years, Roberta would wait until every other student had left the room when a class ended; she did not want people to see her from the back. She even started to wear a cape to school. Although she's now over fifty and her mother has long been dead, her very unhappy physical self-image remains perhaps the largest part of the legacy her mother bequeathed her.

WHEN YOU'VE HUMILIATED ANOTHER PERSON

The great Jewish theologian Rabbi Abraham Joshua Heschel once said, "When I was young, I admired clever people. Now that I am older, I admire kind people." Rabbi Heschel understood that it's a greater accomplishment to be kind than to be brilliant.

Harry Truman might not have been the greatest intellectual ever to occupy the office of president. But in addition to his penetrating common sense, Truman possessed kind instincts, epitomized by the extraordinary care he took not to humiliate others.

In 1962, some ten years after he left the White House, Truman was lecturing before a group of university students in Los Angeles. During the question-and-answer period, a student asked him: "What do you think of our local yokel?" referring to California governor Pat Brown.

Mr. Truman bristled and told the boy he should be ashamed of himself for speaking of the governor in so disrespectful a manner. He continued scolding the boy a while longer; by the time he finished, the student was close to tears.

What marks this story off as different from every other account until now is what happened next: "When the question period was over," writes Merle Miller, author of an oral biography of the president, "Mr. Truman went to the boy and said that he hoped he would understand that what he had said had to do with the principle involved and that he meant nothing personal. The boy said that he did understand, and the two shook hands. Afterward Mr. Truman went to see the dean to ask him to send reports from time to time on the boy's progress in school. The dean said he would. . . . I asked Mr. Truman if he had ever heard from the boy himself, and he said, 'He's written me two or three times, and I've written him back. He's doing very well.'"*10

What makes Truman different from some of the political figures discussed elsewhere in this book is that he had the awareness and sensitivity to realize—not ten years later or even one year later but immediately—that the public scolding he had given the boy, even if the young man's words had been foolish and disrespectful, could subject him to ridicule and contempt. Imagine how different Joanne's life would have been if the teacher who had mocked her, realizing right away the unfairness and evil of what she was doing, had desisted and apologized.

Other observers of Truman have noted that being attentive to others' feelings was very important to him. In 1964, when the newsman Eric Sevareid interviewed him about his presidential experiences, Truman commented: "What you don't understand is the power of a President to hurt."

Sevareid was struck by this remark. "An American President has the power to build, to set fateful events in motion, to destroy an enemy civilization. . . . But the power of a President to hurt the feelings of another human being—this, I think, had scarcely occurred

---

* President Truman's concern about not inflicting gratuitous hurt is confirmed in an anecdote related by Tip O'Neill, the late speaker of the House of Representatives: "I met [President Truman] with a group of us freshmen when I came to Congress in 1953, and the conversation turned to Mamie Eisenhower [wife of the newly elected Republican president]. Truman said that he had no use for Ike. 'But leave his family alone,' the President continued, his voice rising. 'If I ever hear that one of you attacked the wife or a family member of the President of the United States, I'll personally go into your district and campaign against you.'" Tip O'Neill with Gary Hymel, *All Politics Is Local* (New York: Times Books, 1994), 35.

to me, and still less had it occurred to me that a President in office would have the time and need to be aware of this particular power among so many others. Mr. Truman went on to observe that a word, a harsh glance, a peremptory motion by a President of the United States, could so injure another man's pride that it would remain a scar on his emotional system all his life."[11]

GUIDELINES FOR ENSURING THAT YOU DON'T HUMILIATE OTHERS

What was it about Harry Truman that caused him to be so conscious of the damage that words can cause? It wasn't an exceedingly mild disposition, for the many Truman biographies indicate that he was an impassioned man who did have a temper. But even when he expressed anger, what stopped him from humiliating others, or caused him immediately to set out to repair the damage if he feared he had done so, was his conscious internalization of the observation he made to Sevareid: "What you don't understand is the power of a President to hurt."

Change "the power of a President" to "the power of words," and you realize that we all have the ability to shame others.

If you reflect for a few moments, you'll realize how many people you can wound verbally (and perhaps already have): your spouse, parents, other relatives, friends, or people who work for you.

The first step in ensuring that you don't abuse this power is to be aware that you have it; otherwise, you'll feel no need to guard your tongue.

But while the first step must be to recognize the power of words to hurt, such recognition alone is certainly not sufficient to stop us from using words destructively. No doubt many readers have nodded as they have read each episode in this chapter, mentally acknowledging the great cruelty of shaming others. However, unless you make such an acknowledgment *again* and *again*, you will probably forget it, particularly during moments of anger.

A popular British story tells of a very prominent politician who one night, having imbibed too much liquor, stumbled into a heavyset female member of Parliament from the opposition party. Annoyed, the woman said to him, "You are drunk, and what's more, you are disgustingly drunk." To which the British parliamentarian responded: "And might I say, you are ugly, and what's more, disgustingly ugly. But tomorrow, I shall be sober." (The story might well be apocryphal, which is yet another reason to not mention names.)

If you, like the politician in question, have a quick temper and pride yourself on having a sharp wit, it is important that you *reflect again and again on the moral evil of shaming another person.*

For Lee Atwater, it was only when he was lying on his deathbed that it became obvious to him how cruel it was to have mocked one of the most painful episodes in another man's life. I am sure that had Atwater been taught throughout his life *again and again*, as I believe all of us must be taught *again and again*, that humiliating another person is as evil as going up to someone in the street and punching him in the face, he wouldn't have done so in the first place.

Similarly, if my friend Roberta's mother, who jeered at her repeatedly for being overweight, had reminded herself again and again how hurtful her words could be—so much so that, *forty years later*, her daughter still looks contemptuously at herself in the mirror—would she not have learned to curb her tongue? I suspect she would have, for Roberta is certain that her mother loved her, since she expressed many warm feelings toward her daughter on other occasions. Yet because Roberta's mother never learned to reflect on the potentially destructive power of words, she didn't feel the need to restrain her tongue when angry. She went through life like a reckless child playing with a loaded gun and never understood that words are like bullets: the damage they wreak often cannot be undone.

An ancient Jewish teaching observes: "It would be better for a person not to have been born at all than to experience these seven things: the death of his children in his lifetime, economic dependence upon others, an unnatural death, forgetting his learning, suffering, slavery, and publicly shaming his fellow man."[12]

The first six items on this list represent some of the most horrific fates imaginable. Anyone who knows someone who has buried a child realizes that no parent ever fully recovers from such pain. Similarly, the prospect of becoming totally dependent on others or, even worse, becoming another's slave is horrifying. As for "forgetting his learning," we have all heard of people contemplating and even committing suicide after being diagnosed with Alzheimer's disease. Although most people won't take so drastic a step, I suspect that most of us would prefer to die than to go through life with severe brain damage.

It's striking that the Rabbis included "and publicly shaming his fellow man" on the listing of terrible occurrences. Note that they did not say "*being* publicly shamed," but "publicly shaming his fellow man." To the Rabbis, becoming the kind of malevolent human being who humiliates others is as appalling a fate as losing a child—or one's mind.

Why? Every monotheistic faith believes that our mental capacities are God-given and that human beings were brought into this world to do good. If it is wrong to squander the gifts bestowed by God, how much worse it is to turn them to such an evil purpose as deliberately hurting another!

One person who learned quite early in life the cruelty of humiliating another was the future American president Dwight Eisenhower, and the lesson he learned at twenty-two affected his behavior for the rest of his life. The episode, which is not well known, is related by an Eisenhower biographer, Professor Stephen Ambrose:

> *In the fall of 1912, third class cadet Dwight Eisenhower . . . was walking down a hallway at West Point when a plebe [a newly entered cadet], running full speed on some fool errand for an upperclassman, ran into him. Reacting with a "bellow of astonishment and mock indignation," Eisenhower scornfully demanded, "Mr. Dumgard [a generic term for a plebe] what was your P.C.S. [Previous Condition of Servitude]?"*
>
> *Eisenhower then added sarcastically, "You look like a barber."*
>
> *The plebe's face went red. He replied softly, "I was a barber, sir."*
>
> *It was Eisenhower's turn to go red with embarrassment. Without a word, he returned to his room, where he told his roommate, 'I'm never going to crawl [haze] another plebe as long as I live.* As a matter of fact, they'll have to run over and knock me out of the company before I'll make any attempt again. I've just done something that was stupid and unforgiveable. I managed to make a man ashamed of the work he did to earn a living."*

Ambrose concludes: "He never hazed again, and as an adult he never shamed a man (further, he put the military hero George

---

* It would be nice to report that in the more than 100 years since Eisenhower learned about the cruelty of hazing—and the hazing in this case was, relatively speaking, quite mild—hazing has ended, but in fact it has continued at many college fraternities and has led to serious injuries and, on occasion, even death. Hazing almost invariably involves, at the very least, humiliating a person trying to enter a fraternity; as I understand it, and based on the principles outlined in this book, it would be categorically forbidden by Jewish ethics—and I would like to believe by other ethical systems as well.

Patton on probation, postponed Patton's promotion to general, and ordered him to publicly apologize, specifically because Patton had humiliated and slapped a soldier suffering from shell-shock and battle fatigue, and called the man a coward)."[13]

Finally, remember that *it is when you are most upset that you need to consider your words most carefully.* Admittedly, thinking about the consequences of what you say before you say it is particularly difficult at such a time. Rabbi Judah the Prince was so bothered by the smell of garlic that he didn't reflect on the shame that his words might inflict on the person who had eaten it. But while Rabbi Judah was justified in being annoyed at the student's garlic breath, the "punishment" inflicted by his sharp words would have far outweighed the victim's "crime." A more compassionate response might have been to mention the garlic, announce a five-minute break, and ask all the students to wash out their mouths.

An ancient Jewish text asks us to take care not to humiliate others even in far-fetched cases: "If someone was hanged in a person's family, don't say to him, 'Hang up this fish for me,'" lest you trigger that distressful memory or remind others who are present of the shameful event.[14] If we are supposed to be morally vigilant even in such a remote case, how much more careful should we be not to publicly mock someone's bad breath, acne, or lack of good looks.

If you have humiliated another person, of course you should apologize to him or her. But the far more moral thing to do is to exercise restraint *before* you inflict shame, for the greatest remorse and the best will in the world never can erase your words. You can do everything possible to try to minimize their impact, but unfortunately, that is all you can do.

CHAPTER 11

Is Lying Always Wrong?

On the one hand,

Liars share with those they deceive the desire not to be deceived.

—Sissela Bok, *Lying*

On the other hand,

A medical professor asked his class if they thought it appropriate to tell a person that he had an illness from which he would surely die. When the professor made known his opinion that a doctor should always leave a person some room for hope, one student argued that if there was no reason for optimism, the doctor should tell the patient the full and ugly truth. The professor told the student that such an attitude made him unfit to be a physician, and that he should immediately go to the dean's office and tell him that professor so-and-so asked that he be expelled. The devastated student started to leave, but after he had taken a few steps, the professor said, "You don't have to go to the dean's office. I just wanted you to experience for a moment the sense of pain, fear, and hopelessness your patient will feel if you tell him that he is going to die soon and there is nothing that can help him."

—Joseph Telushkin, *A Code of Jewish Ethics*, vol. 1, *You Shall Be Holy*

WHAT WORDS SHOULD people call out as they dance in front of a bride?" With this question, the Talmud inaugurates a strange debate.

The School of Rabbi Hillel answers that wedding guests always should exclaim: "What a beautiful and gracious bride!" The School of Rabbi Shammai disagrees. "If she is lame or blind, are you going to say of her, 'What a beautiful and gracious bride'? Does not the Torah command, 'Stay far away from falsehood'?" (Exodus 23:7). This school thus insists that no standard formula be recited; rather, each bride should be described "as she is."

"According to your words," the followers of Hillel respond, "if a person has made a bad acquisition in the market, should one praise it to him or deprecate it? Surely [you would agree that] one should praise it to him. Therefore, the Rabbis teach, 'One's disposition should always be pleasant with people.'"[1]

This talmudic debate highlights a question that religious and secular thinkers have been considering for millennia: When, if ever, is it appropriate to lie?

A surprising number of ethicists have answered, "Never." Not only would they not sanction the sort of tactful words advocated by Hillel, but they feel it is wrong to lie even when a life is at stake.

The fourth-century Saint Augustine, arguably the preeminent Church Father, is the most forceful Christian advocate of this position. He believed that, since telling an untruth costs a person eternal life, lying to save a life is foolish and unjustifiable: "Does he not speak most perversely who says that one person ought to die spiritually, so another may live? . . . Since then, eternal life is lost by lying, a lie may never be told for the preservation of the temporal life of another."[2]

Augustine's absolutist position influenced some very heroic Catholics to feel that they had behaved immorally because they lied. Father Rufino Niccacci, a peasant priest who saved 300 Jews in Assisi from the Nazis by providing them with forged identity papers and helping them blend into the non-Jewish community, was troubled by the deception in which he had participated: "I became a cheat and a liar, for a good cause, mind you, but nevertheless a sinner, although I am sure that I have long since made my peace with God, and that He has forgiven my trespass."[3] Apparently Father Niccacci—certainly a saintly figure as I understand it—regarded people who refused to tell such lies (and thus save innocent lives) as on some level less sinful than he.

For the eighteenth-century Immanuel Kant, perhaps the modern era's most influential philosopher, telling the truth was a universal moral absolute that allowed for no exceptions. In the essay "On a Supposed Right to Tell Lies from Benevolent Motives," Kant contends that if a would-be murderer inquires whether "our friend who is pursued by him has taken refuge in our house," we are forbidden to lie and mislead him.[4] Kant goes so far as to say that if you respond accurately to the would-be killer's question about the location of his intended victim, you incur no moral guilt for the ensuing murder. However, if you lie to the murderer and say that your friend is no longer home, but unbeknownst to you your friend has gone out, and "the murderer had then met him as he went away and murdered him, you might justly be accused of being the cause of his death. For if you had told the truth . . . perhaps the murderer might have been apprehended by the neighbors while he searched the house and thus the deed might have been prevented. Thus, whoever tells a lie, however well-intentioned he might be, must answer for the consequences, however unforeseeable they were, and pay the penalty for them even in a civil tribunal." (A reader of Kant's essay may feel that, emotionally, Kant seems to be almost as angry at the man who tried to deceive the would-be murderer as at the criminal himself.)

In her book *Lying*, the philosopher Sissela Bok points out that, according to Kant's ethics, a ship captain transporting refugees from Nazi Germany would have been forbidden to lie to the captain of a patrolling German vessel who asked whether there were Jews aboard.[5] Bok's example is apt, for in no country did Kant exert a greater influence than in his native Germany. Yet a German who would have looked to him for moral guidance during the Nazis' murderous rule would have found himself forbidden to lie to Nazi officials in order to save innocent lives.

The Hebrew Bible's view differs sharply from both Augustine's and Kant's. When life is at stake, the Bible depicts God as not only permitting lying but even mandating it. For example, when God commands the prophet Samuel to anoint David as king in place of Saul, Samuel refuses. "How can I go? If Saul hears about it, he will kill me" (I Samuel 16:2).

God neither promises Samuel protection nor tells him to speak truthfully and bear the consequences. Rather, He instructs the prophet to tell Saul a lie—that his trip's purpose is not to anoint a new monarch but to offer a sacrifice. Apparently God wishes to teach Samuel—and all readers of the Bible—that one does not owe the truth to would-be murderers.

What of the more common situation that most of us face—when a life is not at stake, but lying will spare feelings? Imagine Kant at a wedding, speaking to a groom:

"What do you think of my bride, Professor?"

"Well, it is clear from looking at her that you did not marry her for her beauty, and from speaking to her, I can see that she is not in possession of a powerful intellect. Then again, perhaps she is very kind. I cannot say that for a fact, of course, since I spent only a few minutes with her."

"Thank you for being so honest about your observations, Professor, but I want you to know that what you have said hurt me."

To which Kant might well have responded, with words drawn

from his previously cited essay, "Truthfulness in statements . . . is the formal duty of an individual to everyone, however great may be the disadvantage accruing to himself or to another."

Such an "I don't care what the cost is" fidelity to truth creates a very inhospitable dynamic.

Concerning other verbal exchanges, Jewish teachings offer a wealth of advice on when and how it is permissible and even praiseworthy to bend the truth, and when it is forbidden. As an example of when *not* to lie, the Talmud offers the somewhat humorous example of Rav, whose wife would torment him by cooking the opposite of what he requested. If he asked for lentils, she gave him peas; if peas, she gave him lentils.

When his son Hiyya became older and realized what his mother was doing, he would invert his father's requests to her. If Rav told Hiyya that he wanted lentils, the boy would tell his mother that his father had requested peas.

One day Rav said to his son, "Your mother has improved." To which Hiyya responded: "That's because I reverse your messages."

Although appreciative of his son's cleverness, Rav instructed him not to do so anymore, because "it is evil to accustom one's tongue to speak lies."[6]

Rav was willing to forgo the convenience to himself that accrued from his son's lies in order to ensure that the boy grew up to be truthful. The contemporary implication is that we too should be very careful not to accustom a child to lying on our behalf, whether to unwanted phone callers ("Tell them Daddy isn't at home") or ticket agents at movie theaters ("Tell them you're only eleven"). A child raised by his parents to lie and cheat for their convenience will quickly learn to lie and cheat for his own convenience. (The eighteenth-century writer Samuel Johnson noted: "If I accustom a servant to tell a lie for me, have I not reason to apprehend that he will tell many lies for himself.")

According to the Talmud, it also is very wrong for a parent to lie *to* a child. "One should not promise a child something, and then not give it to him, because as a result the child will learn to lie."[7] When a parent promises a gift to a child and does not "deliver," the child may at first be bitterly disappointed, but eventually will conclude cynically that this is how the real world works.

The Talmud emphasizes how very wrong it is to lie or mislead a person in order to secure some personal advantage. For example, it is forbidden to invite someone to be your guest if you know that he or she will refuse, since your goal is to make the person feel indebted or grateful to you for something you never intended to do.[8] Likewise, it is not permitted to open an expensive bottle of wine and tell a guest that you are doing so in his honor when it was your intention in any event to uncork the wine.[9] On the other hand, if the guest drew the wrong inference and said, "I am deeply touched that you served such wonderful wine in my honor," then the guest is misleading himself, a misapprehension that you are not obligated to correct, since doing so would come at the cost of causing him pain.

Indeed, where one's goal is to avoid inflicting gratuitous emotional pain on another, Jewish law becomes remarkably tolerant of half-truths and "white lies." For example, and as noted in chapter 2, Genesis 18 records the visit of three angels to Abraham and Sarah at a time when Abraham was ninety-nine years old and his wife was eighty-nine. The angels tell Abraham that within the year Sarah will give birth. Listening nearby, Sarah laughs to herself, saying: "Now that I am withered, am I to have enjoyment, with my husband so old?"

In the next verse, God asks Abraham: "Why did Sarah laugh, saying, 'Shall I in truth bear a child, old as I am?'" (Genesis 18:12–13). Compare Sarah's words with God's, and you'll note that God doesn't transmit her entire comment to Abraham: he omits Sarah's reference to Abraham being "so old," presumably out of concern that such a comment might hurt or anger him. On the basis of this passage, the Talmud concludes: "Great is peace, seeing that for its sake even God modified the truth."[10]

As a general principle, lying can be considered permissible when the truth can do no good and will only cause pain. Thus, if your spouse is getting ready to go to a party and puts on a dress or a suit that is unattractive and asks how she or he looks, you should respond truthfully. By doing so, you might well save your spouse from embarrassment. But if you meet someone at a party in similarly unattractive clothes and that person asks the same question, it would be pointless, and gratuitously cruel, to answer: "You look terrible," even if that's what you think.

There are a few specific instances when Jewish tradition actively encourages lying. From Judaism's perspective, life is almost always a higher value than the truth, so that, as noted, you certainly do not owe "just the facts" to a criminal who will use them to murder someone. (You're also entitled to lie to a thief concerning the whereabouts of an object he wishes to steal. Particularly when you are dealing with an unscrupulous person, preserving property is sometimes also a higher value than truth.) As we discussed in chapter 2, if an individual asks you what someone has said about her, you're permitted, indeed obligated, to leave out negative comments (except in certain rare cases; see page 37). If the person continues to press you for information ("What else did he say?"), you're permitted, if necessary, to answer, "Nothing else. He said nothing negative." (The exception occurs when what has been said is more than the sort of passing annoyed comment that many of us occasionally make about others and there is a compelling reason why the person needs to know what it is.) Jewish law places one restriction on this rare permission to lie: no one is to take an oath to a false statement, thus committing perjury (which is specifically prohibited by the Ninth Commandment). To swear to something untrue, particularly when invoking the name of God, is never allowed (except when an innocent life is at stake).

Thus, from this perspective, truth is a very important value but not an absolute one, even if Immanuel Kant—who, as far as is known, was never involved in a love relationship, never had children, and had a very low regard for Judaism—felt differently.

While most lying is reprehensible (who wants to be friends with a person whose statements you can't trust, or a person who misleads others to benefit himself?), people who pride themselves on *always* being truthful sometimes use this as an excuse to become verbal sadists. In his autobiographical *A Writer's Notebook*, Somerset Maugham conveys how a cruel truth, told solely to benefit the speaker, wrought an unbearable consequence. A woman who had become pregnant during an adulterous affair waited some thirty years to tell her husband that the son he so cherished was not his. Within days, the man committed suicide. Upon learning of his death, the wife, who was suffering from mental instability and had been told that her husband had died in an accident, said, "Thank God, I told him when I did. If I hadn't, I should never have had another moment's peace in my life."[11]

I would designate such a person a malevolent truth-teller. She didn't inform her husband of her adultery at the time it occurred, perhaps because she wanted to retain the advantages of living with him, as he was a wealthy man. Instead, she waited decades until her husband had forged a very close bond with the child he assumed was his. Now that she was suffering from mental instability, which may have made her incapable of enjoying her life, she wished to see her husband suffer as well. I would argue that telling the truth *at the time she chose to do so* was a worse betrayal than her original act of adultery.

Verbal sadism is common and particularly harmful within marriages. For example, during a time of marital tension, a man I know told his wife about six different women he knew to whom he was more attracted than her, and how much he fantasized about sleeping with them. Likewise, parents who make it clear to their child that they prefer one of his or her siblings are guilty of such sadism.

Not surprisingly, in the talmudic debate that began this chapter, the tradition ends up ruling in favor of Hillel, who advocates praising the bride, in deference to both her feelings and those of the groom. As the hero of Graham Greene's novel *The Heart of the Matter* says: "In human relations, kindness and lies are worth a thousand [gratuitously painful] truths."12

MACRO LIES

Until now, we have focused on "micro" lies—the untruths we tell to protect other people's feelings or safety. My friend Dennis Prager makes the point that while ethical considerations allow some (though by no means all) such untruths, it is impermissible to lie about "macro" issues that transcend the individual.

Macro lies can be particularly pernicious. For example, *The Protocols of the Elders of Zion*, a late nineteenth-century forgery, alleged that there was an international Jewish conspiracy to take over the world and plunge nations into warfare and poverty. The historian Norman Cohn has documented the Nazis' citation of *The Protocols* as a "warrant for genocide" against the Jews. During the Holocaust, six million Jews, of whom over one million were children, were murdered; the *Protocols*' lies helped set the stage for their annihilation.13

By contrast to the Nazis' use of macro lies, people who are motivated by a desire to mobilize large numbers of people on behalf of a noble cause sometimes tell macro lies. But the use of ignoble means to achieve noble ends often results in new forms of immorality. For example, impelled by the desire to rally public opinion against Germany during World War I, Allied propagandists concocted tales of terrible atrocities carried out by German occupation troops. Soldiers were accused of tossing infants into the air and impaling them on their bayonets, cutting off children's hands, and raping nuns. These stories were widely believed and endorsed by, among others, the noted historian Arnold Toynbee.[14] While such lies helped unite citizens of Allied countries and motivate their troops, they also stimulated anti-German hatred and occasionally provoked physical attacks against Americans of German descent.

When World War I ended, it became widely known that although German rule had been harsh and deserved criticism, its soldiers had not carried out the atrocities of which the propagandists had accused them.

Adolf Hitler was among the few people who thought that telling this type of macro lie was a good strategy. He wrote in his political autobiography *Mein Kampf*: "The British and American war propaganda was psychologically correct. By displaying the German to their people as a barbarian and a Hun, they were preparing the individual [Allied] soldier for the horrors of war, and . . . heightened his rage and hatred against the villainous [German] enemy."[15]

More than twenty years later, during World War II, when stories again began to circulate of terrible atrocities committed by German troops, they turned out this time to be all too true. But many people rejected the reports, citing the lies told during World War I. It was argued that once again a similar kind of anti-German propaganda was being spread. Thus, an immoral lie told during World War I was a factor in discouraging people from believing *true* reports of Nazi atrocities in World War II. If more people had believed what the Nazis' victims were saying, greater efforts on their behalf might have been undertaken.

Undoubtedly, the creators and disseminators of World War I anti-German propaganda felt that it was noble to lie on behalf of a worthwhile cause. They were wrong, however, and more than two decades later tens of thousands of innocent victims may well have paid the price for their moral error.

People's tendency to tell untruths or spread absurd exaggerations—or simply to be extremely sloppy in their fact-checking—is perhaps most disturbing when they're espousing high-minded causes. An unfortunate example of this occurred in the late 1980s and early 1990s. Many feminists as well as others who were not feminists, including many who were not even women, justifiably felt that American society had put great and unfair emphasis on women being thin, and they regarded the eating disorder anorexia nervosa as one perverse consequence of this. Unfortunately, in their desire to grab the attention of listeners and readers and alert them to the disease's horrors, some leading feminist writers seem to have concluded that provoking and infuriating their audience was more important than fact-checking.

In *Revolution from Within*, Gloria Steinem, writing in 1992, informed readers that "in this country alone . . . about 150,000 females die of anorexia each year."[16] If accurate, this figure would have meant that more than one million American women had died from this eating disorder during the preceding seven-year period, that more Americans died from anorexia than from strokes, and that in any given year almost four times as many American women had died from anorexia as the total of all people who had died in car accidents. (In 1992, 39,250 Americans were killed in car accidents.)

Steinem cited Naomi Wolf's best-selling book *The Beauty Myth* as a source for her statistic. The number of alleged deaths from anorexia, and the sufferings of its victims, had so shocked Wolf that she felt compelled to note that, although "nothing justifies comparison with the Holocaust . . . when confronted with a vast number of emaciated bodies starved not by nature *but by men*, one must notice a certain resemblance."[17]

Wolf, in turn, cited as her source the book *Fasting Girls: The Emergence of Anorexia Nervosa as a Modern Disease* by Joan Brumberg, a historian and the former director of women's studies at Cornell University. In a book that received four major awards and was hailed by the highly regarded *Journal of Social History* as a "masterful blend of history and contemporary issues," Brumberg posited that these 150,000 annual deaths were due to "a misogynistic society that demeans women . . . by objectifying their bodies."[18] Therefore, it was allegedly men, the creators of the "misogynistic society that demeans women," who were responsible for the deaths of these tens of thousands of women. Brumberg attributed the statistic to the American Anorexia and Bulimia Association.

The philosophy professor Christina Hoff Sommers, author of *Who Stole Feminism?*, was puzzled by this statistic. If over a million women had died from anorexia in the preceding seven years, how was it possible that she didn't know many of them—or even any of them? One wonders whether the same question hadn't occurred to Brumberg and the writers who cited her. As of 1994, around the time these books were written, fewer than 300,000 Americans had died from AIDS, yet obituaries for the disease's victims frequently appeared in newspapers. Very rarely, if ever, did one read of a woman succumbing to anorexia. (A rare exception was Karen Carpenter, lead singer of The Carpenters.)

When Sommers contacted Dr. Diane Mickey, the American Anorexia and Bulimia Association's president, she learned that its carefully researched statistics had been seriously altered, distorted, or, at the very least, grossly misinterpreted. In a 1985 newsletter, the association had written that 150,000 to 200,000 American women suffered from anorexia nervosa. This figure represented the sum total of American women *afflicted* with the disorder, not the number who *died* from it annually.

According to the Division of Vital Statistics of the National Center for Health Statistics (NCHS), 101 women died from anorexia nervosa in 1983, and 67 died from it in 1988. The NCHS reported 54 deaths from anorexia in 1991 (and none from bulimia)—or *about one-three-thousandth of the number reported by Brumberg and cited by Steinem and Wolf.* Concludes Professor Sommers: "The deaths of these young women are a tragedy, certainly, but in a country of one hundred million adult females, such numbers are hardly evidence of a 'holocaust.'"[19]

Today it is now clear that thousands of women—an estimated 8,500, according to Johanna Kandel, the founder and CEO of the Alliance for Eating Disorders—die annually from a variety of diet-related causes.[20] This is a tragedy of enormous proportions that must and is being addressed by organizations such as the Alliance. However, it is equally clear that the claim that 150,000 were dying annually in the United States from anorexia never bore *any* relationship to reality.

Yet, unfortunately, once best-selling authors introduce such "facts" to hundreds of thousands, if not millions, of readers, their data, and the conclusions resulting from them, become widely accepted. In April 1992, Ann Landers wrote in her syndicated advice column: "Every year, 150,000 American women die from complications associated with anorexia and bulimia." *The Knowledge Explosion,* a university textbook for women's studies courses—published by Columbia University's Teachers College Press—also contained this figure in its preface.

The spreading of such highly exaggerated statistics—indeed, the distortion is so mammoth that the word "exaggeration" seems an understatement—leads not only to excessive alarm about a dreaded disease but also to great anger at men. After all, it is men, and the beauty standards they have supposedly conditioned women to strive for, that are responsible for the alleged deaths of 150,000 women annually (which works out to more than 400 deaths a day).[21]

In conclusion, macro lies and grotesque exaggerations are wrong, morally wrong. If you believe that telling such untruths—or being very incautious in ascertaining whether your statistics are correct—is the only way you can buttress an argument, consider whether your cause is just and persuasive enough not to have to rely on distortions of the truth. As Friedrich Hebbel, a nineteenth-century German playwright, wisely observed: "One lie does not cost you one truth, but the truth."

CHAPTER 12

Not Everything That Is Thought Should Be Said

It's so simple to be wise. Just think of something stupid to say and then don't say it.

—Sam Levenson

NOT ALL HURTFUL speech is said by people who intend to cause pain, a fact that does not necessarily lessen the hurt. This was brought home to me some years ago when I was writing an ethics advice column on the website beliefnet.com. One of the very first letters I received was the following:

Dear Joseph,

At a party a few months ago, when I was barely beginning to come to terms with the reality that my two-month-old baby was born with a severe disability, I mentioned my situation to another guest at the party. She replied, "You must be a very nice person—I don't believe that God would give such a baby to someone who wasn't good enough to take care of him." I was stunned, hurt, appalled, angry. I thought, "No,

God doesn't work that way—He wouldn't do that to me." I wanted to put her in her place but was too taken aback, and, despite my fury, worried that I'd show my bile to someone who was probably well intentioned. What should I have said to her?

"Did this woman have good intentions?" I began my response. She probably did, I acknowledged, but what she unfortunately lacked was common sense—both about God and about another person's feelings. Analyze exactly what it was that she was saying. First, she supposes that she knows God's will. But how does she know why God sent this mother a baby with a disability? A medieval Jewish proverb teaches, "If I knew God, I'd be God." This woman doesn't know God and isn't God. And if she were God, she might well discourage people from being good by making it known that the better they were, the more likely it was that God would send them babies with disabilities.

Like many well-meaning but verbally impulsive people, this woman probably spoke without thinking—without first considering the profound pain her listener was feeling and how her words might be heard. Or she might have been one of those people who becomes very uncomfortable with silence and feels that *something* must be said, even if it turns out to be inane or worse. I suggested to the letter writer that if she could explain to the woman why her comment was wounding, she might realize her error, apologize, and, most important, refrain from hurting people with comments like this one in the future. Perhaps, I suggested, she could have said to her something like this: "I know you meant well, but you should know that your words hurt me. For one thing, the implication of your comment—if only I were a less nice person, I would have had a baby without severe disabilities—is a very painful thought. How would you feel if someone said to you, 'You seem like such a nice person that I pray God will reward you by causing you to have many babies with special needs.'"

The truth is that this woman was mouthing what I would call "a pious platitude." Her comment put me in mind of an incident recounted by the twentieth-century Jerusalem sage Rabbi Shlomo Shwadron. Rabbi Shwadron once saw a child get injured while playing in the street. He lifted the bloodied boy and started running to a nearby hospital. An older woman, seeing the very worried look on the rabbi's face, called out to him, "Don't worry, Rabbi. God will take care of everything."

As Rabbi Shwadron passed her, the woman recognized the child he was carrying as her own grandson. "Isaac, Isaac," she started shrieking hysterically, and she yelled after the rabbi, "Is he going to be all right? Is he going to be all right?"

For many people, like this grandmother, pious-sounding statements when other people are suffering cost nothing and mean nothing. It is like reassuring a person in desperate need of money, "God will provide." Or saying to someone who has suffered a tragic loss, "Whatever God does is for the best." Anytime you are tempted to utter a platitude, think instead, *What would I want someone to say to me if it were my child or grandchild who was injured and in danger?* It is quite likely that, other than, "What can I do to help?," there is nothing else you would want another person to say to you.

When Robert Kennedy Jr. eulogized his beloved friend Eric Breindel, he recalled the message that Breindel had left on Kennedy's answering machine some months earlier when Kennedy's brother, Michael, had died: "Tell me where to go, and what to do, and I will be there."

Fourteen words, all of them one syllable, but these were the words that Kennedy chose to recall in his eulogy.

In brief, words other than the most basic aren't always necessary, and when they aren't necessary, they can be hurtful—as in the case of the woman who felt impelled to offer a rationale to the woman who had given birth to a baby with disabilities.

One of the most profound and most ignored biblical verses is from the third chapter of Ecclesiastes, which notes that there is "a time for silence and a time for speaking."

"A time for silence." It is to such people as the woman who purported to know God's will that the following words from Rabbi Israel Salanter are directed: "Not everything that is thought should be said." Sometimes all that is required from us is that we listen and empathize. That is the brilliance—and I use the word advisedly—of the Jewish law ordaining that when people enter the house of a mourner, they say nothing but wait until the mourner speaks. The visitor cannot know what the mourner most needs at that moment. For example, the visitor might feel that he or she must speak about the deceased, but the mourner—who might have been speaking about the deceased nonstop for several hours already—might feel too emotionally overwrought or drained to do so at that moment. Conversely, the visitor might try to cheer up the mourner by speaking of a sports event or some other irrelevancy at just the moment when the mourner's deepest need is to speak of the dead. And of course the mourner might just want to sit quietly and say nothing at all.

My friend Rabbi Jack Riemer was with Rabbi Abraham Joshua Heschel when they heard of the death of the sister of their mutual friend, Rabbi Wolfe Kelman. Rabbi Heschel insisted that they go to visit Rabbi Kelman and his family members immediately: "We went to the airport, we flew to Boston, got into a cab, and went to the house," Rabbi Riemer told me. "Heschel walked in, he hugged the mourners, he sat silently for an hour. He didn't mumble a single cliché, [like] 'How old was she?' [What difference does it make?] [or] 'I know how you feel' [You don't know how I feel]. None of the clichés. He just sat there in silence for an hour. And then he got up, hugged them, and we left. I learned that you don't have to be glib. You just have to care."

The guidance provided here—to know when to say nothing—applies to micro events, such as the death or suffering of an individual. Maintaining silence or minimizing one's words applies equally when a macro tragedy occurs. Some people—a fair number of them clergy—feel the need to offer an explanation for why tragedy occurs, even if they have to contort one to fit in with what they already believe. In the aftermath of 9/11—the day in 2001 when Islamist terrorists murdered almost 3,000 Americans in New York, in Washington, D.C., and on four airplanes—the Reverend Jerry Falwell suggested that God had withdrawn protection from America and allowed this attack to happen because the United States was permitting abortions, homosexuality, and secular schools. Falwell's explanation not only offered no comfort to people mourning the deaths of parents, children, spouses, and friends but actually made many people angry at a God who would punish people with such fates. (Shortly thereafter, the Reverend Falwell apologized for his remarks.)

In a comparable manner, there were prominent rabbinic scholars in the aftermath of the Holocaust who, in effect, blamed the Jewish victims for their own sufferings. Commenting on the large and growing number of Eastern European Jews who had become irreligious, one prominent rabbi wrote that God sent "Hitler's demons to end the existence of these communities before they deteriorated entirely."[1]

The cruelty—and I would argue absurdity—of explaining the Holocaust as either a punishment directed against Jews for their sinfulness or a preventive measure to keep them from becoming even more irreligious enraged Rabbi Yitz Greenberg, a prominent modern Orthodox rabbi: "Now that [the victims of the Holocaust] have been cruelly tortured and killed, boiled into soap, their hair made into pillows and their bones into fertilizer . . . and the very fact of their death denied to them [by Holocaust deniers], the theologian would inflict on them the only indignity left; that is, insistence that it was done because of their sins."[2]

The bottom line is this: don't speak as if you know when you don't know. Don't tell a mother trying to come to terms with the birth of a child with severe disabilities why God sent her such a baby, and don't tell people who have suffered tragic losses that you know why they have suffered such a loss.

The oft-ignored aphorism "think before you speak" is always applicable. Say nothing to another person unless your words will be healing, or at least helpful. Perhaps the smartest advice I have ever heard on this subject comes not from a religious text or a philosopher, but from the American comedian Sam Levenson, whose comment opens this chapter: "It's so simple to be wise. Just think of something stupid to say and then don't say it."

PART FOUR

THE POWER OF WORDS TO HEAL

CHAPTER 13

Words That Heal—and the Single Most Important Thing to Know About Them

THE MOST IMPORTANT thing to know about words that heal is not that they be eloquent, but that they be said.

GRATITUDE

If your friend did you a small favor, let it be in your eyes a big favor.

—*The Fathers According to Rabbi Nathan* 41:11

To become adept at saying "thank you," one must first cultivate gratitude—the Hebrew phrase for which, *ha-karat ha-tov*, literally means recognition of the good another has done for you.

Sometimes gratitude can be expressed by a simple "thank you," but other times it is expressed by a lifetime of devotion.

Leopold Pfefferberg was one of the 1,100 Jews whom Oskar Schindler saved during the Holocaust. In 1947, just before Pfefferberg and his wife emigrated from Germany, he promised Schindler that he "would make his name known to the world." A short time later, when he learned that Schindler was impoverished, he helped raise $15,000 for him, a substantial amount of money in the late 1940s.

In 1950, Pfefferberg (who subsequently changed his name to Page) moved to Los Angeles and opened a leather-goods store in Beverly Hills that was patronized by many prominent Hollywood actors, writers, and producers. He tried to interest them all in Schindler's story. On one occasion, when the wife of a prominent movie producer brought in two expensive handbags for repair, he told her, "If you let me talk to your husband about this story, you won't have to pay a penny for repairing the bags." The husband came in, and Pfefferberg told him about Schindler. Intrigued, the man wrote a treatment for a film, but unfortunately no studio was interested in producing it.

Pfefferberg was undaunted; throughout the 1960s and 1970s, he continued to tell everyone he could about Oskar Schindler. One day in October 1980, the Australian novelist Thomas Keneally came into his store to buy a briefcase. When Pfefferberg learned that Keneally was a writer, he immediately started telling him Schindler's story and urged him to write a book about it.

Keneally listened attentively to Pfefferberg's recitation. He agreed that the story deserved to be told, but added, "I am not the man who can write this book for you. I was only three years old when the war started, so I don't know too much about it. Second, I am Catholic and don't know much about what happened to the Jews during the Holocaust."

Fearful that yet another opportunity to fulfill his thirty-three-year-old vow to the now-deceased Schindler would be lost, Pfefferberg was not dissuaded. "I was a teacher," he told Keneally, "and I lived through it. I will tell you everything I know. With a little research, you will be as educated as anybody about this period of history. As an Irish Catholic and notable author, you will have more credibility, not less, in writing about the Holocaust."

On the spot, Keneally committed himself to writing the book. In 1982, *Schindler's List* was published to international acclaim. Pfefferberg subsequently served as a technical consultant to Steven Spielberg's 1994 Academy Award–winning film of the same title.

The promise that a grateful Leopold Pfefferberg made to Oskar Schindler in 1947 had at last been fulfilled. A man who also understood the meaning of gratitude, Keneally dedicated *Schindler's List* to Leopold Pfefferberg. And Steven Spielberg, also intent on expressing gratitude, concluded his film at the Catholic cemetery in Jerusalem, where he showed the surviving remnant of "Schindler's Jews" gathered around the righteous man's grave to honor his memory.

Of course, expressions of gratitude are usually carried out on a less grand scale. The Talmud teaches that "one who learns from his companion a single chapter, a single law, a single verse, a single expression, or even a single letter, should accord him respect."[1] In fulfillment of this teaching, when the third-century rabbinic sage Rav heard that his earliest childhood teacher had died, he tore his garment as a sign of mourning.[2] This act may seem exaggerated, but to one who appreciates the meaning of gratitude, it makes considerable sense. If you enjoy reading and appreciate that much of what you have been able to achieve in life derives from your literacy, then don't you owe a lifelong debt of gratitude to the person who taught you how to read? (See the story on pages 6–7 about the letter that the Reverend William Stidger wrote to an elementary school teacher who had encouraged and inspired him decades earlier.)

Jewish tradition ordains that a Jew should thank God with a hundred blessings every day. Although such a large number of blessings might strike some as "too much," a person who habituates him- or herself to reciting blessings learns not to take life's pleasures for granted. Not only should we thank God, but we should likewise not take for granted the pleasures that others have provided for us.

The Talmud speaks of the second-century rabbi Ben Zoma, who was grateful even to people he had never met but who had enriched his life. As Ben Zoma put it: "What labors did Adam [the first man on earth] have to carry out before he obtained bread to eat? He plowed, he sowed, he reaped, he bound the sheaves, threshed the grain, winnowed the chaff, selected the ears, ground them, sifted the flour, kneaded the dough, and baked. And only then did he eat. Whereas I get up and find all these things done for me."[3]

Ha-karat ha-tov means thanking the taxi driver who has driven well, acknowledging the waitress who has served you efficiently and pleasantly, appreciating the clothing salesman who helped you choose garments you will now be proud to wear, and expressing gratitude to the bank official who has fulfilled a complex transaction graciously. Of course, gratitude should not be restricted to strangers. Indeed, how much more gratitude do we owe to those who give meaning to our lives—our spouses, our parents, our children, our friends, our relatives?

Rabbi Jack Riemer has shared with me one of his favorite poems, the anonymous "Things You Didn't Do."

> *Remember the day I borrowed your brand new car and dented it?*
> *I thought you'd kill me—but you didn't.*
> *And remember the time I dragged you to the beach, and you said it*
>   *would rain, and it did?*
> *I thought you would say, "I told you so"—but you didn't.*
> *And remember the time I flirted with all the guys to make you*
>   *jealous—and you were?*
> *I thought you'd leave me—but you didn't.*
> *And remember the time I spilled blueberry pie all over your brand*
>   *new rug?*
> *I thought you'd drop me for sure—but you didn't . . . .*
> *Yes, there are lots of things you didn't do,*

But you put up with me, and you loved me, and you protected me;
And there were so many things I wanted to make up to you when you
returned from the war—but you didn't.

IN PRAISE OF PRAISE

A biblical law ordains: "You shall not cheat a poor or destitute laborer . . . On that day [of his labor] you shall pay his hire: the sun shall not set upon him, for his life depends on it. Let him not call out against you to God, for it shall be a sin upon you" (Deuteronomy 24:14–15).

Withholding payment to day laborers is profoundly harmful; they are not people with deep resources, and their very lives may well depend on it. Rabbi David Ingber suggests expanding the scope of this law. He notes that the withholding of compliments and affirmation is also very wrong. Of course, words of acclaim are not actual payment, but words of praise can become a tangible, spiritual payment. It has been repeatedly documented that though many employers think that what matters most—and perhaps exclusively—to workers is salary, employees consistently report that what matters to them even more is acknowledgment and appreciation.

The Bible records that when Moses told his Midianite father-in-law, Hobab (more commonly known as Jethro), that he and the Israelites were journeying to the land promised them by God and invited him to come along, Jethro declined, saying he wanted to return to his native land. "Please do not leave us," Moses said. "You know where we should camp in the desert, and you can be our eyes" (Numbers 10:31). Jethro did indeed choose to return to his native land, but is there any doubt that he left this encounter with the greatest leader of his age feeling valued and fully appreciated?

Another law in the Bible rules that one is obligated to reprove another when one sees the other person doing something wrong (Leviticus 19:17). But isn't an upshot of that law that one should praise another when one sees them doing something right? If you are a person who writes letters of complaint when you feel you have received bad service, then make sure you also write letters praising employees who have treated you well. It is unjust and unfair to be quick to criticize but slow to offer a good word.

The withholding of praise can have other devastating effects. "I know a man," Rabbi Harold Kushner writes, "a successful business executive, who works twelve hours a day, six days a week, to make his business even more successful than it already is. He doesn't have to do it. He is financially secure; his company will certainly continue to be successful for the foreseeable future. . . . Why does he continue to work so hard? Because his father was a successful businessman, and my friend lives for the day when he will hear his father tell him, 'I'm proud of you; you're as good as I ever was.' My friend wears himself out to earn that compliment, but he will never hear it. His father has been dead for fifteen years.

"My friend has never been able to get over the fact that when he was a child, he was never sure how much his father loved him. He was taught that love had to be earned, 'You'll have to do better than that if you expect me to be satisfied.'"[4]

Strangely enough, there is also something self-serving in being generous with praise: "Whenever we reward a person with gratitude and kind words, the person who is rewarded will repeat that behavior."*

---

* I have heard variations of this comment but have not been able to locate a source.

Studies have shown that foster-care children who are raised in homes where they are given little attention or recognition eventually stop creating pictures or building with Legos.

"Praise is to children," Rabbi Ingber says, "as water and light are to trees and plants."

A Postscript Regarding Husbands, Wives, and Gratitude

Just as I was preparing to submit this manuscript for publication, I came across an extraordinary idea from Lord Jonathan Sacks, the Chief Rabbi Emeritus of the British Commonwealth and one of the most knowledgeable and creative thinkers in the Jewish community today. The idea had been prompted by something Rabbi Sacks learned from the speech therapist Lena Rustin.

> *From time to time couples come to see me before their wedding. Sometimes they ask me whether I have any advice to give them as to how to make their marriage strong. In reply, I give them a simple suggestion. It is almost magical in its effects. . . . They have to commit themselves to the following ritual. Once a day, usually at the end of the day, they must each praise the other for something the other has done that day, no matter how small; an act, a word, a gesture that was kind or sensitive or generous or thoughtful. The praise must focus on that one act, not [be] generalized. It must be genuine: it must come from the heart. And the other must learn to accept the praise. That is all they have to do. It takes at most a minute or two. But it has to be done, not sometimes, but every day.*[5]

WHEN SPEAKING TO THE VULNERABLE
(AND WE ARE ALL VULNERABLE)

As noted, the most important thing to say about words that heal is that they be said.

Consider the case of Rachel Naomi Remen, a shy and somewhat insecure child. Remen's parents, both highly accomplished professionals, were devoted to her, yet her parents' house was the sort where her father would comment if she came home with a 98 on a test: "What happened to the other two points?"

"I pursed those two points relentlessly throughout my childhood," Dr. Remen, a physician, recalls in her memoir *My Grandfather's Blessings*. However, there was one person who didn't care about those two points—her grandfather. Every Friday after school she would go to his house and spend the afternoon with him. The two would talk, drink tea together, and then, as the sun went down, her grandfather, a religious man, would light two candles and recite a blessing over them to inaugurate the Sabbath. He would then sit quietly for a few moments, having a silent conversation with God. The young Rachel would wait patiently because she knew the best part of the week was coming. After a minute or two, her grandfather would ask her to come over to him.

> He would rest his hands lightly on the top of my head. He would begin by thanking God for me and for making him my grandpa. He would specifically mention my struggles during the week and tell God something that was true. If I had made mistakes during the week, he would mention my honesty in telling the truth. If I had failed, he would appreciate how hard I had tried. If I had taken even a short nap without my nightlight, he would celebrate my bravery in sleeping in the dark. Then he would give me the blessing and ask the long-

ago women I knew from his many stories—[the matriarchs]
Sarah, Rebecca, Rachel and Leah—to watch over me.[6]

To this day, Remen recalls those moments as the only time in the week when she felt completely safe and at rest.

The saddest event of Remen's childhood was her grandfather's death when she was only seven. It was hard for her to live in a world bereft of him. "At first I was afraid that without him to see me and tell God who I was, I might disappear. But slowly over time, *I came to understand that in some mysterious way, I had learned to see myself through his eyes.* And that once blessed, we are blessed forever."[7]

Decades later—and to Remen's great surprise—her mother, then in deep old age, began to light Sabbath candles. On one of those occasions, Remen told her about the blessings her grandfather had given her and how much they had meant to her. Her mother smiled at her sadly: "I have blessed you every day of your life, Rachel," she told her. "I just never had the wisdom to do it out loud."

By definition, healing words must be spoken. Hugs are appreciated, but certainly not as meaningful as Remen found her grandfather's words to be.

For Alan Dershowitz, it was not a grandfather but an altogether different sort of mentor—a kind that any one of us could be to another—who uttered the words that forever transformed the young man's vision of himself.

Dershowitz has, of course, long been among America's best-known attorneys. A lawyer who has tried many of the country's most famous cases, Harvard Law School's most famous professor, the author of dozens of books, a public figure, and the holder of controversial views he is never afraid to espouse, Dershowitz is about the last person one would imagine grew up with serious issues of self-confidence. Yet he did. "I was fifteen years old before anyone told me I was smart," Dershowitz recalls in his book *Letters to a Young Lawyer.*

He was a bit of a smart-aleck as a kid, as well as an indifferent student consumed with sports, girls, and joking around with friends. Neither of Dershowitz's parents had gone to college, and he grew up assuming that he would eventually end up like his dad, selling men's clothing: "I didn't see how history or spelling would make me a better salesman," so why waste time, he figured, studying when "scoring a basket or flirting with girls could gain me immediate gratification." More often than not his grades were C's.

Then one summer well into his high school years, Dershowitz worked at a children's camp as a waiter. He soon found himself having serious conversations with the camp's drama counselor, a man in his early twenties: "We had long conversations about religion, philosophy, literature, drama, and of course girls." One day the counselor, Yitz Greenberg, just blurted out, "You know, you're really smart." Dershowitz was taken aback. "I knew he meant it because he wasn't the flattering type and anyway, why would he need to flatter me? *His statement changed my life.* It gave me the confidence to act as if I were smart, despite my lingering doubts." A year later Dershowitz graduated from high school and entered Brooklyn College, where he "went from being a C student to an A student."[8]

I remember how struck I was when I read that story, and I reread it several times. I know Yitz Greenberg. During my undergraduate years at Yeshiva University, he was my favorite and most influential professor. Years later, he was the rabbi who performed the wedding when Dvorah and I married. And of course, he has over the past decades been one of the most influential thinkers in Jewish life.

I knew many things about Yitz Greenberg, but the story of those five words was not something I had known. Even now, more than sixty years after that conversation, Dershowitz continues to insist, *"His statement changed my life."*

We all know of instances where words have changed people's

lives for the worse—verbal abuse heaped on children and spouses, the internet bullying of young people (some of whom are even driven to suicide), the taunting of African Americans with cruel epithets. That we have the power to use words to change people's lives for the better is among the most precious gifts human beings have been given.

STEPHEN CARTER, A professor of law at Yale University Law School, has long been one of America's premier public intellectuals. Over the past decades, Carter's books—among them *Integrity*, *Civility*, and *The Culture of Disbelief*—have helped shaped public debates and discussion on many of the most pressing issues confronting the United States.

A distinguished African American academician, Carter writes in an engaging style devoid of academic jargon. Indeed, it is in just such language that Carter relates an incident from his childhood that forever changed his life.

Carter was a young boy when he and his family moved from a black to a white neighborhood in Washington, D.C. The young Carter was uncomfortable about the move—and with reason. Sitting on the front steps of his new house with his brothers and sisters, "we waited for somebody to say hello, to welcome us. Nobody did . . . I knew we were not welcome here. I knew we would not be liked here. I knew we would have no friends here."

But Carter's fears and trepidations were set at ease by one person who, it turns out, was a religious Jew:

> All at once, a white woman arriving home from work at the house across the street from ours turned and smiled with obvious delight and waved and called out, "Welcome!" in a booming confident voice I would come to love. She bustled into her house, only to emerge, minutes later, with a huge

tray of cream cheese and jelly sandwiches, which she carried to our porch and offered around with her ready smile, simultaneously feeding and greeting the children of a family she had never met—and a black family at that—with nothing to gain for herself except perhaps the knowledge that she had done the right thing. We were strangers, black strangers, and she went out of her way to make us feel welcome. The woman's name was Sara Kestenbaum, and she died much too soon, but she remains, in my experience, one of the great exemplars of all that is best about civility. . . . She managed in the course of a single day, to turn us from strangers into friends, a remarkable gift that few have. . . . To this day, I can close my eyes and feel on my tongue the smooth, slick sweetness of the cream cheese and jelly sandwiches that I gobbled on that summer afternoon when I discovered how a single act of genuine and unassuming civility can change a life forever.[9]

Carter's vulnerability was understandable: he was a young black child feeling unwelcome in an overwhelmingly white neighborhood. The truth, however, is that all of us are vulnerable, to different degrees and at different times. Ralph Branca was a young pitcher on the Brooklyn Dodgers. In 1947, at the age of only twenty-one, he won twenty-one games—in a sport where any pitcher who won more than twenty games in a season was a star. Two years later, Branca had a winning percentage of .722, an astounding statistic. But in 1951, with one pitch, Branca became associated forever with what may have been the most catastrophic loss any major league team has ever experienced.

A few days earlier, the Brooklyn Dodgers and the New York Giants (now the Los Angeles Dodgers and the San Francisco Giants) had ended the baseball season in a tie for the pennant. They then entered into a three-game playoff for the National League championship. The teams split the first two games, and in the third game the Dodgers were leading in the bottom half of the ninth 4–2. The Giants had two men on base, and Branca was brought in to pitch to the Giants outfielder Bobby Thomson. Branca needed to secure just two outs to win the pennant for the Dodgers. But then, on Branca's second pitch, Thomson smacked the ball into the stands for a three-run home run. With one hit—forever immortalized as "the shot heard round the world"—Thomson had captured the pennant for the Giants and become an overnight hero. And with one pitch, Branca had lost the pennant for the Dodgers and become an overnight goat.

When Branca came into the Dodger clubhouse, the players were stunned. In those days, baseball salaries were much lower and the earnings from the World Series could come close to equaling a full season's paycheck. No one said a word to the clearly grieving Branca, who was lying down and crying. Then one man, Jackie Robinson, the most famous Dodger and baseball's first African American player, came over to Branca. "Don't take it personally," Robinson said to Branca, sweet words but words that were hard to take seriously. How could Branca not take this catastrophe personally? Then Robinson added a few more words, and it was these words that Branca said he remembered for the rest of his life. "If not for you, we would not have gotten this far."

"If not for you, we would not have gotten this far."

Could those words take away all the pain? Of course not. But they reminded Branca that he could not define his entire life by one unfortunate play, terribly hurtful as it was. And the fact was that the Dodgers had gotten as far as they had due in large measure to the hours upon hours of great pitching from Branca.

Robinson not only had the kindness to say these words but the wisdom to know the words that could help console at a moment of such pain. It is not enough to want to be good; good intentions are important but not sufficient. Goodness often requires wisdom as well, something Jackie Robinson had in abundance.

Offering words that heal is not only about complimenting people's attainments, as Robinson did when he spoke of Branca's extraordinary pitching, but also about offering, at the right time, the words that people most need to hear. And certainly when speaking to people in vulnerable situations, the right words are essential. Benji Levene tells of an incident that occurred more than fifty years ago, one whose message still resonates. At a synagogue in Jersey City, the long-serving Rabbi C. Y. Bloch had died, and sometime later Rabbi Chaim Jacob Levene applied for the position that was now open. The search committee chose Levene, and when the committee chairman called to tell him the news, the rabbi thanked him, but said that he would need a week before he could give a definite answer. The chairman was puzzled, but granted the rabbi's request. Finally, at the end of the week, Rabbi Levene answered that he would accept the position. It was only years later that his son, Benji, learned the reason for his father's delay.

"It was my father's custom," Benji Levene recalled, "after we had settled into the community to visit the widow of Rabbi Bloch every Friday morning, and sometimes he would take me along." The two would walk up several flights of stairs to Mrs. Bloch's apartment, where Rabbi Levene would engage her in conversation and inform her of some of the goings-on in the community. Once, when his father had an errand to run, he excused himself and left his son with the widow. Benji Levene remembers that Mrs. Bloch gave him cookies and a soda, and then said, "I am going to tell you a story, which I don't want you to ever forget.

"When your father was asked to accept the position of rabbi here, he said that he needed a few days before he could give the committee an answer. Do you know why he did that? It was because he first wanted to come to see me.

"When he came in, he said, 'I know for many years you were the first lady of the congregation, and I understand that it will be difficult for you, after all these years, to see someone else take your husband's place. The board has offered to make me the next rabbi, but I have not given them an answer yet. I wanted to see you first, in order to ask your permission. If you want me to take the position, I will, but if in any way you feel that you don't want me to be here, I will leave right away.'"

"The widow told me that at that moment, she started to cry, and she said to my father, 'Now that my husband is gone, who is there who cares about me or thinks that what I feel is important? I am so touched that you came here today to ask my permission.' And then she paused, 'I told him, not only do I want you to stay and be the rabbi, but now I feel as if my own son were taking the pulpit.'

"'Then,' she continued, 'only then did your father go back and accept the position. And for the first year, he did not sit in the rabbi's seat on the pulpit in the synagogue, in deference to my husband's memory. And he never told anyone what I have just told you.'"

Years later, Benji Levene insists that "my father's behavior in this incident—more so than any book of ethical instruction I have read—remains for me the archetype of how a rabbi should act . . . in fact, how all human beings should treat one another."[10]

MORAL IMAGINATION

Over the past century, there have been extraordinary advances in medicine, science, and technology. These advances have come about because a scientist or group of scientists used their intellectual imagination to resolve problems that had been thought to be insoluble. When it comes to moral improvement, however, advances have been more checkered. Some very important improvements have been made, most notably the acquisition of greater rights for women, African Americans and other minorities, and the physically and mentally disadvantaged. On the other hand, the twentieth and twenty-first centuries have witnessed the greatest mass murders in history, most notably the Nazi Holocaust, the tens of millions murdered by bloody Communist tyrants such as Stalin in Russia, Mao Zedong in China, and Pol Pot in Cambodia, and the butchering of almost a million Tutsi in Rwanda.

How do we account for the great advances in science and medicine and the much more tentative advances in morality? One explanation, I suspect, is that while many scientists and inventors devote the full resources of their intellect and imagination to seeking solutions to scientific problems, people rarely devote the full resources of their moral imagination to finding solutions to moral issues.

One person who did so was Rabbi Shlomo Zalman Auerbach (1910–1995). Based in Jerusalem, Rabbi Auerbach was one of the great rabbinic scholars of the twentieth century. His ingenious solution to one dilemma that came before him reminds us that *even when we think nothing can be done to improve a situation, that might well be because we are just not thinking hard enough.*

What happened in this case was that the concerned parents of a mentally challenged child came to Rabbi Auerbach to consult with him on the choice of a residential institution for their son. They were deciding between two facilities, each one having certain advantages over the other. Rabbi Auerbach listened carefully to the parents' description and then asked, "Where is the boy? What does he say about all this?"

The parents looked at one another in astonishment. They conceded that it had never occurred to them to discuss the matter with their son. "And frankly," the father added, "I don't see much point in discussing it. This is not something he can grasp."

Rabbi Auerbach was irate: "You are committing a sin against the soul of this child!" he cried. "You intend to evict him from his home and consign him to a strange place with a regimented atmosphere. He must be encouraged and not be allowed to feel that he is being betrayed." The parents were speechless.

"Where is the boy?" Rabbi Auerbach demanded. "I would like to see him and discuss the matter with him personally."

The couple hurried home and returned with their son.

"What is your name, my boy?" Rabbi Auerbach asked.

"Akiva," the child replied.

"How do you do, Akiva. My name is Shlomo Zalman. I am the *Gadol Ha-dor*, the greatest Torah authority of this generation,* and everyone listens to me. You are going to [choose and] enter a special school now, and I would like you to represent me and look after all of the religious matters in your new home."

The boy's eyes were riveted on the rabbi's face, and the awestruck parents sat with their mouths agape as the Rav continued. "I shall now give you *semicha* [ordination], which makes you a rabbi, and I want you to use this honor wisely."

Rabbi Auerbach gently stroked the child's cheek and saw that he was as eager as could be to fulfill his part of the agreement. Over the years, on numerous occasions when this youngster was to spend a Shabbat at home, he refused to leave the institution, insisting that, as the local rabbi, he had a responsibility to his constituents. After all, he had been charged with this responsibility by none other than the greatest rabbi of the generation, the *Gadol Ha-dor*![11]

Moral imagination is what enabled Rabbi Auerbach to grasp that what the parents were doing could have inflicted a lifelong trauma on a young and very vulnerable child (feeling exiled from

---

* Reb Shlomo Zalman was exceptionally humble and normally never referred to himself, or permitted others to refer to him, by such a title.

the only home he had ever known), and moral imagination is what enabled the sage to come up with a solution that filled the child's life with dignity.

Moral imagination can be exercised by children no less than by adults. Ian O'Gorman, a ten-year-old boy in Oceanside, California, was diagnosed with cancer. The doctors prescribed ten weeks of chemotherapy, during which, they warned him, all his hair would fall out. To avoid the anxiety and pain of watching his hair gradually disappear, the youngster had his entire head shaved.

One can only imagine Ian's feelings a few days later when he returned to school, prematurely bald, and was greeted by the thirteen other boys in his fifth-grade class, and their teacher as well, with their heads completely shaved.

What an eloquent statement of empathy! When the desire to ease someone else's pain is sufficiently deep, one can almost always find words or deeds that will make a difference.

There are many ways to show our loving feelings. In her influential best-seller *You Just Don't Understand: Women and Men in Conversation*, Deborah Tannen tells of her widowed great-aunt, who had a love affair while already in her seventies. Although she was overweight and her hands and legs were misshapen by arthritis, she had fallen in love, with a man also in his seventies.

In describing to her great-niece what the relationship meant to her, the elderly woman recounted that she had gone out with friends for dinner and, when she returned home, her male companion telephoned. When she described the dinner to him, he listened with interest, then asked, "What did you wear?"

Recalling this question, Tannen's great-aunt started to cry. "Do you know how many years it's been since anyone asked me what I wore?"

"When my great-aunt said this," Tannen concluded, "she was

saying that it had been years since anyone had cared deeply, intimately, about her." Because her great-aunt's companion cared deeply, he could find and express the words that made her feel loved.[12]

Such was the case as well with Joe Lapchick, one of the great basketball players in the pre–World War II era. Lapchick played center for the legendary Original Celtics. When his young son was stricken with polio, Lapchick's neighbors expressed concern for the seven-year-old boy's health. The basketball star was shocked, however, when one of them, in the presence of the sick child, asked "if the boy would ever be able to play basketball again."

The next day, when he visited the hospital, he asked his son if he wanted to be a basketball player. The boy said yes, and his father told him that all he wanted was for him to have a happy and normal life and to give something back to society.

The son eventually recovered and fortunately suffered no long-term effects from his illness. Years later, however, he still recalled the words his father had spoken to him that day in the hospital. As the son of a great athlete, he had always imagined that he had to follow in his father's footsteps. His father's words, which conveyed a love not conditioned on his son replicating his feats, freed the young boy from the assumption that he too had to be a sports star: "I recognized . . . that my father had given me perhaps his greatest gift on that morning in Grasslands Hospital. He freed me of the need to please him and gave me the opportunity to fulfill myself."[13]

Moral imagination likewise enabled the grandmother of Allen Sherman, the comic songwriter, to soothe the heart of the young Sherman when he was feeling deeply humiliated after making a miscalculation and being laughed at by his mother. Much later, Sherman would be reminded of that earlier incident when he thoughtlessly hurt the feelings of his own young son. He had been in the middle of an intense conversation with his wife when his son entered to show off a drawing he had just finished. Sherman, annoyed at having his conversation interrupted, quickly dismissed the childish scrawls. Hurt by his father's rejection, the boy threw the drawing down on the floor, rushed up to his room, and slammed the door.

The slamming of the door reminded the now-abashed Sherman of a door that he himself had slammed twenty-five years earlier. One morning he had heard his Yiddish-speaking grandmother announce that she needed a "football" for a large party she would be hosting that evening. Although the young Sherman wondered why his grandmother needed a football, he was determined to procure one for her. He went around his neighborhood and finally found one boy with a football, although the boy was a bully who punched him in the nose before agreeing to give over his football in exchange for Sherman's best toys.

Sherman took the football home, polished it until it shone, and left it for his grandmother. His mother saw the football first, however, and became upset with him for leaving his toys around. When he explained that it was for his grandmother's party, his mother burst into laughter: "A *football* for the party? Don't you understand your own grandma? Not a football, a *fruit bowl*. Grandma needs a fruit bowl for the party."

The embarrassed boy ran up to his room, slammed the door, and refused to come down to the party. But a little later his mother came up to fetch him. When she brought him downstairs, he saw his grandmother proudly walking around the room with a large bowl filled with a variety of beautiful fruits and, in the middle, the polished football he had brought home. When a guest asked his grandmother to explain what a football was doing in the middle of the fruit bowl, she told him about the gift from her grandson and added, "From a child is beautiful, anything."[14]

WHEN THE HARSHEST WORDS
ARE THE MOST BLESSED

Perhaps the most unusual story I have ever come across on the ability of the right words to comfort, and in this case to save, is one that I learned from Rabbi Lawrence Kushner. Kushner himself heard this story from a rabbinic student, Shifra Penzias, whose great-aunt Sussie was a young Jewish woman living in Munich in the 1930s after the Nazis' rise to power. Sussie was on a bus when SS storm troopers boarded the vehicle and began examining people's identification papers. Jews were told to get off the bus and go into a truck around the corner.

The young woman watched as the soldiers started to systematically work their way down the bus. She began to tremble, and tears started to stream down her face. The man alongside her saw her crying and politely asked her why.

"I don't have the papers you have," she answered. "I am a Jew. They're going to take me."

"The man exploded with disgust. He began to curse and scream at her. 'You stupid bitch,' he roared. 'I can't stand being near you.'"

The SS men came over and asked what all the yelling was about.

"Damn her," the man shouted angrily. "My wife has forgotten her papers again! I'm so fed up. She always does this."

The soldiers laughed and moved on.

"My student said that the great-aunt never saw the man again. She never even knew his name."[15]

Obviously few of us will ever find ourselves in a position where the right words might save another's life (and put ourselves in danger) or save another person from irrevocable pain and suffering. But we can be influenced to become better people just by reading such stories and resolving that if we ever encounter such a situation, or even a far milder situation, we will use the full resources of our intellect and of our courage to help another.

In the case of Ford Frick, the National League president from 1934 to 1951 (and subsequently the commissioner of Major League Baseball), the situation he confronted in 1947 was not as dangerous as the one confronting the young woman on the bus, but it was very explosive and demanded wisdom and courage. That year Jackie Robinson had become the first black man to play on a major league team, and word reached Frick that a group of players on the St. Louis Cardinals were trying to organize a strike among their teammates: the players were going to refuse to take the field if the Dodgers showed up with Robinson in uniform. Frick realized that the whole future of black players in baseball—as well as the moral credibility of both baseball and, in some ways, the United States—was at stake. He therefore decided to confront the Cardinal players in the most direct manner possible and with the most confrontational words he could summon:

"If you do this," Frick informed the players, "you will be suspended from the league. You will find that the friends you think you have in the press box will not support you, that you will be outcasts. I don't care if half the league strikes. Those who do will encounter quick retribution. They will be suspended and I don't care if it wrecks the National League for five years. This is the United States of America, and one citizen has as much right to play as another.

"The National League will go down the line with Robinson whatever the consequence. You will find that if you go through with your intention that you will have been guilty of madness."

Roger Kahn, author of *The Boys of Summer*, notes that after Frick's statement, "Robinson's road, although still steep, led from thicket to clearing."

Healing words, as this case makes clear, might not always be healing for the person or persons to whom they are directed, but they can be very healing for the victims of abuse (such as Jackie

Robinson). And sometimes they even serve as a favor to the people who are acting abusively by stopping them from engaging in immoral behavior (which, for the St. Louis Cardinals planning to strike, would have destroyed their professional lives).

Such is the case with an incident that I learned about from my friend, the psychiatrist Dr. Stephen Marmer, who shared a treasured memory from his days in medical school:

"When I was a second-year student, during one particular lecture, a student rose to ask a very elementary question. The teacher glared and replied: 'That is a stupid question!' The red-faced student sat down, but another student, one of the best in the class, raised his hand. Expecting a more intelligent comment or question, the teacher recognized him. The second student proceeded to say, 'Professor, none of us in this class is stupid. We may be ignorant, but that is why we are here to learn. You should apologize to so-and-so and to the class.' At that point, all the other students applauded. To his credit, the professor did offer an apology before continuing his lecture, and even thanked the admonishing student."

This incident remained a formative one in Dr. Marmer's own development: "I have never forgotten how morally courageous that was for my classmate to do."

"I'M SORRY"

We have all heard of feuds between siblings or close friends that have lasted for years but could have been brought to an immediate end if only one side had said, "I'm sorry." Yet, for many people, those two words are the hardest words to say. Apologizing means acknowledging that you have been wrong, perhaps even cruel.

If I seem to be exaggerating when I say that a simple apology could *often* defuse even a long-standing fight, then think of someone who has made you angry. If that person suddenly came to your house and sincerely expressed his remorse and sorrow at the hurt he has caused you, would you really remain unmoved?

According to an ancient Jewish teaching, a person who sincerely repents on Yom Kippur (the Day of Atonement) will be forgiven for any sins he has committed against God. But the Day of Atonement cannot bring about forgiveness for sins committed against another person until you go to the person you have hurt and apologize.

One of my own profound experiences with apologies occurred between myself and one of my daughters and oddly enough led to one of the funniest experiences in my life, if a slightly embarrassing one. At the time, our family was living in Boulder, Colorado, and I was invited to give a talk on the ethics of speech in nearby Denver. My daughters Naomi and Shira, who were then six and four, said they wanted to attend my speech. "We know you give speeches, Daddy, and we want to come." Frankly, I was concerned that the talk would be way over their heads and boring to them. Nonetheless, they kept insisting they wanted to come and so I brought them.

I'm a proud father, and at the beginning of the speech, I introduced them to the audience of several hundred people; the people clapped loudly, and Naomi and Shira went to sit down in the front row.

About ten minutes into the speech, I asked the audience, "How many of you grew up in a household where somebody's bad temper had a bad effect on the family?"

Among the hands that went up—to my acute discomfort and to the immense amusement of the audience—was that of Naomi, soon followed by that of Shira. The audience's laughter was uproarious, and I finally said the only thing I could say, "Unfortunately, my wife has a bad temper."

In actuality, I had undertaken to teach Naomi how to read because she was attending first grade at a school that very much took its time in teaching the basics. (The school didn't want to pressure the children in any way, and Naomi spent much of her time drawing.) According to my wife, I am very patient the first time I explain something to someone, and I am also very patient the second time. By the third time, however, if I think the person should have understood what I am explaining, I can become snappy. And apparently I had sometimes been snapping at Naomi when she made reading errors.

After the speech, I went over to Naomi and said to her, "I apologize. When you make a mistake, you are not doing it to be bad, and it is wrong for me to get annoyed at you. Please forgive me." I also told her that if I did so again in the future, she should say, "Daddy, you're not supposed to get angry if I make a mistake." Which she did (and which, I confess, could sometimes be a little annoying).

I have frequently told this story to emphasize to parents that if they act unfairly toward their children, they are obligated to apologize to them, just as they would be obligated to apologize to anyone toward whom they have acted unfairly. Parents who don't apologize to children when they should are communicating an awful, though likely unintentional, message to their children—that you only have to apologize to those who are stronger than you. Because what other lesson can children deduce if, when their parents act wrongly toward them, they don't apologize? The psychotherapist Terry Wohlberg notes that apologies convey another important message as well: by making it clear that it is okay to admit when you have made an error, an apology models for children how to act in a relationship. Apologies also communicate that anger or conflict do not have to threaten a relationship.

Obviously, the ability and willingness to apologize is vital in all our dealings, not just with children, and is usually the only way to bring peace to a troubled relationship. The expression "I beg your forgiveness" is a revealing one. Begging is a humiliating activity.

The thought of having to go out into the street, for example, and plead with passersby for money would horrify most people. I remember that when I was a child the word often used interchangeably with "beggar" was "bum."

Generally, when we have hurt someone, the pain they have experienced at our hands in some way humiliated them, and there is therefore a certain poetic justice in our having to "beg" forgiveness and undergo a certain, albeit small, measure of humiliation ourselves.

An illuminating example of a wrongdoer's willingness to undergo a degree of humiliation occurred some years ago in baseball. Yogi Berra, the star New York Yankees catcher and later manager, was going through a rough stretch as a manager in 1985 when, only sixteen games into the season, Yankees owner George Steinbrenner sent a team executive with a message to Berra that he was fired. Berra, long known for his consistent good cheer and warmth, was extremely hurt, but not so much because he'd been fired; after all, he had been fired before. Rather, what pained Berra so deeply was that Steinbrenner didn't deign to deliver the news personally; Berra, in response, vowed never to set foot in Yankee Stadium as long as Steinbrenner owned the team.

Fourteen years later, as Dr. Aaron Lazare, a psychiatrist, relates in his book *On Apology*, Steinbrenner showed up at Berra's house, took his hand, looked him in the eye, and said, "I know I made a mistake by not letting you go personally. It's the worst mistake I ever made in baseball."

As deeply hurt as Berra had been by Steinbrenner's earlier action, this clearly heartfelt and sincerely expressed apology melted his heart. Berra, in turn, responded with extraordinary graciousness: "George, everyone makes mistakes."

At that point, Steinbrenner said that if Berra would be willing to come to Yankee Stadium, he would personally bring him across the George Washington Bridge in a rickshaw.[16]

The two men's reconciliation eventually became total, and their relationship grew into a substantial friendship over the coming years. All this would never have happened if Steinbrenner had not taken that first, admittedly difficult, step of seeking out Berra and apologizing.

Like all healing words, apologies don't have to be long, as this story and the story of my apology to my daughter illustrate. They just have to be offered, they need to be sincere, and they should also be specific, with a precise acknowledgment of what the wrongdoer did.[17]

In Dr. Lazare's book, a remarkable collection and analysis of apologies, he records a short apology that ended a long feud. After Lazare had delivered a lecture on this very subject, a seventy-three-year-old retired machinist came up to him and told Lazare of his own experience: "I worked at my machine for thirty years. One day, something happened between me and the fellow next to me. Some unpleasant words were exchanged. I do not remember what was said or who was at fault, but we stopped talking. We did not speak to each other for the next six years. One day, I turned to him and said, 'I have been a damned fool,' and I stretched out my hand for him to shake. We shook hands. The grudge was over. Several workers nearby came over and asked what was going on. I said: 'I don't have to be a damned fool all of my life.'"[18]

Like many fights, the reason for the two men's estrangement was so trivial that the machinist could not recall what had triggered the initial fight. (That's why it was sufficient for him to say, "I have been a damned fool.") Nor is it even clear that the machinist who offered the apology bore all the responsibility for the conflict and the ensuing years of hostility. But by humbling himself and calling himself a fool, he "returned respect and esteem to the other party." Once this dignity was restored, the other man, I suspect, could recognize that he too probably bore some responsibility for the fight and the lengthy estrangement.

Apologies, including brief apologies, can work even when the reason for the ill will is far more substantial. In 1916, when President Woodrow Wilson nominated Louis Brandeis to serve on the Supreme Court, former president William Taft was livid. He held back none of his anger, writing that Brandeis's nomination was "one of the deepest wounds that I have had as an American and as a lover of the Constitution . . . [the very idea] that such a man as Brandeis could be on the Court." He lambasted Brandeis as a man "prompted by jealousy, a hypocrite . . . who is utterly unscrupulous . . . and a man of infinite cunning . . . and, in my judgment, of much power for evil." Taft mobilized opposition to the nomination, and eventually he, along with six other former presidents of the American Bar Association, sent a letter to the Senate Judiciary Committee declaring that Brandeis was "not a fit person to be a member of the Supreme Court of the United States."

This intense opposition notwithstanding, Brandeis's nomination was approved. Several years later, Brandeis was taking his pre-dinner walk when "a portly gentleman bumped into him and then stopped short. Brandeis looked up, and before he could say anything, the heavyset man offered his hand and said: 'Isn't this Mr. Brandeis? I am Mr. Taft. I once did you a great injustice, Mr. Brandeis. I am sorry.' 'Thank you, Mr. Taft,' Brandeis responded."[19]

Taft subsequently offered a more expansive apology to Brandeis, requesting forgiveness for his tirade against Brandeis's nomination and for the American Bar Association letter. When Taft was appointed chief justice in 1921, he and Brandeis, despite their ongoing political and judicial differences, developed a very real friendship. In 1923, after two years on the Court together, Taft wrote his daughter Helen, "I have come to like Brandeis very much indeed."

HAVING NOTED SEVERAL episodes of brief apologies leading to reconciliation, I know that there are hurts and injustices that cannot be rectified by a simple apology. (For that matter, I don't know how forgiving Brandeis would have been if Taft's denunciation of his character had succeeded in permanently destroying his good name and keeping him off the Court.) But in many of the conflicts in which most of us are engaged, a relatively few words of true regret can help. For most people, holding on to a grudge is not pleasant—as I once heard someone put it, "Holding on to a grudge is like allowing the person in the world whom you most dislike to live in your mind rent-free"—and offering an apology, particularly if it is accepted, is emotionally satisfying both for the one who offers it and the one who receives it. And even if your apology is not accepted, you are no worse off than before you offered it.

One principle, however, should always be remembered: when you offer an apology, it must be one-sided—you must assume full responsibility for the hurt that was inflicted. Imagine if George Steinbrenner had qualified his words when he came to Yogi Berra's house: "I'm sorry the way I handled your firing, Yogi, but you have to admit you were having a terrible season, and I just couldn't stand it anymore." Do you think such words would have restored to Yogi Berra his wounded dignity and enabled him to truly welcome Steinbrenner back into his life?

Or imagine if the old machinist had turned to the man working alongside him and said, "This is ridiculous. We have both been acting like fools, and if you are willing to shake my hand, I am willing to regard the conflict as over."

Or imagine if I had said to my daughter, "I'm sorry I have snapped at you, but you have to admit it's pretty irritating when you make the same mistake over and over."

In all such cases, and in almost all cases in which an apology is required, the party offering the apology has to assume full responsibility. Ironically, it is precisely that assumption of responsibility that enables the other party not to react defensively but to acknowledge when appropriate his or her own role in either starting or continuing the conflict.

Besides assuming responsibility, you should also not try to minimize what you have done. When someone says, "I am sorry if you felt hurt by what I said," the clear implication is that the person who was hurt is overly sensitive. To restore dignity to the person whose feelings were hurt, you have to specify what you did wrong and make the person who has been hurt feel whole again.

In short, the words "I'm sorry," followed by a statement of the wrong that you have done, almost always work—and certainly where the hurt has not been irrevocable.[20] As noted earlier, just think of how you would react. If somebody who has hurt you comes and begs forgiveness, wouldn't that usually soften your hurt and end your anger?

A final thought: Put down this book for a moment now and think of someone you might have hurt, intentionally or unintentionally. If you are ready to do so, give the person a call and say, "I'm sorry."

If you are unwilling to do this, ask yourself why. Does it make sense to go on with the quarrel? Does the reason for the fight still seem as monumental as when it first occurred? If it doesn't, perhaps the time has come to write an email or a letter of apology, or to call that person up and tell him, "I'm sorry for what I did. I'm sorry for our fight, and sorry for our lost years of friendship."

WORDS THAT CAN MAKE CHILDREN MOST LOVE THEMSELVES—AND OTHERS

A lot of things that are wrong with the world we can't fix by ourselves. As much as we would like to see peace brought to troubled areas, corrupt governments reformed, and cancers cured, there is a limited amount that any of us can do as individuals about such things. However, there is one thing that nearly all of us can do that will immediately and exponentially increase goodness and happiness on earth.

Parents—and all other adults—should reserve their highest praise of children for when they do kind acts. This is not the case at present. As a rule, children receive their highest compliments for one of four things:

- Their intellectual and academic achievements ("My son Sean is brilliant! His teacher says he is the best student she has had in years.")

- Their athletic abilities

- Their artistic achievements ("Sarah is just an extraordinary dancer.")

- Their looks (particularly for girls)

Everyone loves compliments, and children who receive their parents' and other adults' compliments in these areas are usually delighted by the praise. But what about the child who doesn't excel at academics? Or the one who isn't a gifted athlete, dancer, or pianist? Or the child who is not particularly attractive?

What will their parents praise them for? The most flattering remark such a child is likely to hear their parents tell others will be something like, "But she is a really good kid." From which it can generally be inferred that being a good kid is no big deal—that, from the parents' perspective, the child is probably not very good at anything worth bragging about.

Some parents to whom I have made this proposal have told me

it's unnecessary; they are certain that they have successfully communicated to their children that being a good person is what really matters most to them.

By and large, these parents are deluding themselves, and there is a way for them to find out if this is so.

For many years, Dennis Prager has suggested that parents ask their children, "What do you think that I, your mother (or father), most want you to be? Successful, smart, good, or happy?" Many parents who have conducted this experiment have been quite surprised to learn that their children usually did not think that being good was what mattered most to their parents.

Try it yourself. Ask your child of any age that question. "What do you think I most want you to be? And what aspect of who you are do you think I take greatest pride in?"

I want to make it clear that I am not suggesting that parents stop complimenting their children for their accomplishments. All children want to know that their parents have respect for their achievements. And girls even more than boys—but boys too—also need to feel that they are physically attractive.

But—and this is an important "but"—what I am suggesting is this: all of the traits that we often emphasize and praise are important, but *only* if being a good person is placed at the top of the list.

You might say, "Don't these traits—academic, athletic, and cultural success—have a value in and of themselves independent of goodness?"

The answer, I believe, is no. They don't. Germany did not start World War II and carry out the Holocaust because it lacked intelligent or cultured people; it contained such people in abundance. What it lacked was enough good people.

Now, what do I mean when I speak about young people being good? Let me cite a few examples:

- Speaking out against and confronting a school bully

- Befriending a new kid at school who isn't popular

- Finding a wallet or cell phone and making every effort to locate the owner instead of keeping it

- Offering his seat on a bus to an older person

- Treating her siblings decently

And much more.

Why will reserving your highest praise for your children's goodness and integrity have so powerful an impact?

Because if all parents started reserving their highest praise of their children for when their children do kind acts, we would raise a generation of people who most feel loved and proud, and who most love themselves, when they are doing kind acts. The self-esteem of children raised in such households will derive from seeing themselves as good people, and that's the self-esteem that matters more than any other. Or to put it another way, *these children's self-esteem will come more from their goodness than from anything else.*[21]

What a world that would be.*

A brief illustration. The well-known sports writer Phil Arvia

---

* A related idea, drawn from Fred Gosman's *How to Be a Happy Parent* (New York: Villard, 1995): "When our kids are young, many of us rush out to buy a cute little baby book to record the meaningful events of our young child's life. . . . But I've often thought there should be a second book, one with room to record the moral milestones of our child's life. There might be space to record dates she first shared or showed compassion or befriended a new student or thought of sending Grandma a get-well card or told the truth despite its cost" (129). Imagine how much any of us would treasure having such a book recording events from our own childhood.

recalls that his father was not overly expressive with emotions or with words. Arvia always trusted his father's love, but he also knew that his father, who needed to be asked for a hug, saw him as the "sensitive" child.

Some of Arvia's fondest childhood memories are of going to Chicago White Sox games with his brother and dad; it seemed as if his father, who had gone to White Sox games in his own childhood, would melt a little at the ballpark and become more open. Of all the games Arvia attended at Comiskey with his father, the one that most remains with him is a game that took place on Bat Day, an annual event when thousands of fans, particularly the young ones, were given real baseball bats just for showing up.

That year Arvia, his brother, and his dad were accompanied by a work buddy of his father's who had brought along his two young children to their first baseball game. Arvia, who knew the stadium well, seems to recall every detail of that day: "[My brother] and I were old pros by then, Comiskey veterans. We were ready to show these rookies the wonders of Comiskey—the gaping window at the back of the outfield stands that bathed you in a cool breeze and let you look down on the hardball courts [and] the ramp in center field where you could look right into the bullpen.

"But even before the game started, it happened. The coworker's kids went off to find a bathroom, only to come back in tears.

"Some older kids stopped them. The crowd, as usual for a Bat Day, was huge and there weren't enough bats to go around. Taking in the story between stifled sobs, we gathered that the big kids asked if they could see the bats, grabbed them, then ran off, blending into the crowd.

"My brother and I looked at each other. We looked at our dad. We handed the two crestfallen kids our bats.

"A few innings later, after his buddy and the kids went off in search of a hot dog or something, my dad stunned me.

"I've never been prouder of you boys," he said.

As Arvia recalls, "I don't remember asking for the hug my dad gave us that day."[22]

POSITIVE THINKING, POSITIVE WORDS, AND THE AVOIDANCE OF NEGATIVE LANGUAGE

Much language that was used in the past was cruel and insensitive, and I am not only referring to racial, ethnic, and religious slurs. My mother, Helen Telushkin, who was born in New York City in 1912 and grew up in the 1920s, recalled hospitals being named "Home for the Incurables." There were both Jewish and Catholic hospitals so named, and I assume there were other such hospitals as well. My mother told me, with some embarrassment, that it was only as an adult that she realized how cruelly demoralizing such a name was. Imagine being a patient in a hospital and being told, "We're moving you tomorrow to the Montefiore Home for the Incurables."

It is for understandable reasons, therefore, that much of what was written in the past on the ethics of speech focused far more on the power of words to harm than to heal. Speaking ill of others, as noted throughout this book, is designated as *lashon ha-ra*, literally "evil tongue," but there is no comparable Hebrew idiom for good, affirmative speech (which can be rendered in Hebrew as *lashon ha-tov*, a term that is rarely used, however).

Regarding unfair speech directed against others—be it through rage, cruel criticism, or words intended to humiliate—there is a Hebrew term, *ona'at devarim*, meaning "oppressing with words." But here, too, there is no widely used Hebrew term for *healing* with words.

While researching a biography I wrote several years ago of Rabbi Menachem Mendel Schneerson, the widely known Lubavitcher Rebbe, I was deeply impacted to learn how opposed he was to the use of all demoralizing language. For example, the Rebbe launched a campaign to influence hospitals (and health care providers) in Israel to stop using the Hebrew term *beit cholim*, which literally means "house of the sick," and has traditionally been the only Hebrew word for hospital. The Rebbe urged them to call themselves instead *beit refuah*, or "house of healing." As he wrote to Professor Dr. Mordechai Shani, a medical ethicist and later the director of the Israeli Ministry of Health: "Even though this would seem to represent only a semantic change, the term [house of healing] will bring encouragement to the sick, and represent more accurately the goal of this institution which is to bring about a complete healing. Therefore, why call it by a word that doesn't suit its intentions?"* The Rebbe understood that the mind-set shaped by encouraging words ("house of healing" instead of "house of the sick") could set the tone for the physician and play a crucial role in the patient's healing. (How much better to be told "Tomorrow you are being sent to a 'house of healing'" than "Tomorrow you are being sent to a 'home for the incurables'"? In any case, today—though not in the 1960s and 1970s—the importance of the patient's mind-set is universally accepted).

The Rebbe was committed to finding a positive approach and positive language even in contexts in which others could only see the negative. And not in a Pollyannaish way either. For example, soldiers in Israel who have been badly and permanently injured in Israel's wars are known as *nechei Tzahal*, "handicapped of the Israeli

---

* It took years, but the Rebbe's efforts eventually bore fruit; today many hospitals in Israel have been renamed or are commonly referred to with some variation of *beit refuah*. Even some Israeli governmental health agencies have changed their names; for example, Kupat Cholim Maccabi (the Maccabi Fund for the Ill) was renamed Maccabi Sherut Briut (Maccabi Healthcare Services), while the Kupat Cholim Clalit, (the General Fund for the Ill) became Sherutei Briut Clalit (General Health Services).

army." On the one hand, the term seems to be factual and to make sense, as it is applied to people in wheelchairs or people who are disfigured or are missing limbs. Yet when the Rebbe met with a group of such soldiers in the years following the 1973 Yom Kippur War, he told them that injuries, even grievous injuries, in no way limited one's spiritual growth; indeed, it can stimulate it. Furthermore, it is also true that many handicapped people develop skills that they would never otherwise have developed.

It has been well documented, for example, that blind people often develop more acute hearing and notice things that sighted people don't, and there have been many people—you can see their work on Google and YouTube—without arms who have produced extraordinary paintings using their feet and mouths. In other words, handicapped people often develop highly impressive talents. The Rebbe was challenging the prevailing, and still present, tendency to define handicapped people only by what they lack; why not, the Rebbe repeatedly emphasized, focus on their strength of spirit, their unusual attainments, and/or the skills that they might well develop? The Rebbe declared to the wounded Israeli soldiers that day: "I therefore suggest that you should no longer be referred to as 'disabled [or handicapped] veterans,' but as '*exceptional* veterans,' which more aptly describes what is unique about you."

To gauge the striking nature of the Rebbe's words, it is necessary to set this incident within its historical context. At the time this meeting happened, and even more so in the preceding decades, physical and other handicaps were commonly described in terms that easily could demoralize the people who had them. An American soldier who had lost both arms in World War II recalled in a memoir that an army doctor—practicing a version of what is known as "tough love"—telling him and other badly wounded and soon-to-be-released soldiers: "This year you're a hero. Next year you'll be a disabled veteran. After that, you're a cripple."

Contrast the effect of sending somebody out into the world with the words "You're a cripple" with the Rebbe's approach: "You're exceptional."

Throughout history, it hasn't only been physically handicapped people who have suffered from being labeled with harsh, demoralizing words. In the 1950s and 1960s, it was still common to use words such as "moron," "idiot," and "retarded"—all of which originated as technical and scientific terms—as contemptuous expressions with which to describe people with disabilities or with which to taunt others. ("What are you, a moron?" I remember hearing children yelling on the playground.) Children with mental deficiencies were commonly dismissed as "retards" and spoken of as if this word alone could fully define them. In those days, no one would have thought to refer to a child with lowered capabilities in some areas as a "child with special needs."* Few people thought of such children as "special" in any way; rather, they were commonly regarded as burdens to be endured.

Here, too, the Rebbe cautioned not to label people with words that, in effect, defined and limited them. When asked to send a message to the Jewish communal conference "On Issues and Needs of Jewish Retarded," the Rebbe noted his objection to that final word: "I prefer to use some term such as 'special people,' not simply as a euphemism, but because it would more accurately reflect their situation, especially in view of the fact that in many cases the retardation is limited to the capacity to absorb and assimilate knowledge, while in other areas they may be quite normal or even above average."

An area in which the Rebbe particularly emphasized that chil-

---

* While acknowledging how pleased the Rebbe would have been with the more refined and positive manner in which people now speak of those he referred to as "special people," I wonder whether the Rebbe would have approved of the now common term "special needs." "Special," of course, is a positive term, but the Rebbe might have questioned the emphasis on "needs" rather than on "potential."

dren with mental challenges should be more aptly regarded as "special" was in matters of the spirit. When a father, Cantor Joseph Malovany, spoke to the Rebbe about his autistic son who was residing in an institution, the Rebbe reminded the understandably upset father that the fact that a person is autistic—suffering from a disease that severely limits one's ability to interact with others—doesn't mean that such people don't "relate to anyone. They might not relate easily, or even almost at all, to people, but to God they relate as well as everyone else, and [sometimes] even more so. While they're not busy with people, they're busy with God." The Rebbe's more positive take on this difficult condition caused Malovany to recall his success in training his son to say a blessing. He then also noted that his son had learned to perform other religious rituals, and that they were very precious to him. The Rebbe urged Cantor Malovany to go further and to put a charity box in his son's room. "It would benefit your son to deposit charity," the Rebbe said, "and when people visit him he will remind them that they must give charity."[23] I can think of few people who would have thought to empower an autistic child living in a clinical environment with the mission of making a positive impact on society as a charity collector.

My own life as a writer was changed by one teaching of the Rebbe in the use of words. He avoided words that had negative connotations or associations. Thus, no matter how great the pressure to finish a project, he never used the word "deadline." Learning of this, I stopped using the word "deadline" myself—not a small achievement for a writer who is constantly working under time pressures and constraints—and came up with the substitute term that I now use, "due date." A small but crucial difference. "Due date" enables me to focus on my excitement about that on which I am working, while "deadline" evokes a feeling of pressure, and even dread. The reason is obvious: "deadline" connotes death, but "due date" suggests birth and new life.[24]

The Rebbe's systematic and persistent emphasis on positive thinking and positive language—going back to the 1960s and even earlier—was a behavioral breakthrough decades ahead of its time, just as some psychologists, most famously Professor Martin Seligman, have been breaking new ground in American life by emphasizing positive language and positive psychology.*

"Think good and it will be good," the Rebbe liked to quote his ancestor, the Tzemach Tzedek, the third Rebbe. Conversely—though the Rebbe did not say this, for he refrained from all negative formulations—"Think bad and it will likely be bad." Why is that? Thomas Friedman has pointed out that even if pessimists have often been right and optimists often wrong, one fact cannot be denied: "All great changes have been accomplished by optimists." And invariably, *optimism starts with words.*

DIAMONDS POLISHED HERE: HOW AN ELOQUENT THOUGHT HELPED TRANSFORM A LIFE

I have emphasized here that the most important thing about "words that heal" is not that they be eloquent but that they be said. And that, of course, is true. But still, there are times when a thought

---

* Over the past decades, Seligman has shaped a whole discipline in psychology, positive psychology. Through books such as *Authentic Happiness* (New York: Free Press, 2002) and *Learned Optimism* (New York: Alfred A. Knopf, 1991), Seligman has made clear the need for a new approach to dealing with the human psyche. He opens *Authentic Happiness* with this observation: "For the last half-century, psychology has been consumed with a single topic only—mental illness." After noting how significant psychology's advances have been in dealing with and relieving depression, schizophrenia, and alcoholism, Seligman then notes how limiting an agenda confined to treating mental ill health can be: "People want more than just to correct their weaknesses. They want lives imbued with meaning" (*Authentic Happiness*, page xi).

phrased in an original way can make the recipient of your words see their own life in a new and different manner—causing that person to change, even radically, as a result.

The psychiatrist Dr. Abraham Twerski, a specialist in addictive behavior as well as a rabbi, recalls an instance when he was speaking at a halfway house in Israel before a group of ex-convicts in recovery. Twerski was talking about the importance of self-esteem when one of the men, Avi, interrupted him: "How can you talk to me of this? I've been in and out of jail for half of my thirty-four years. I've been a thief since I was eight. When I'm out of prison, I can't find work and my family doesn't want to see me."

Twerski interrupted and asked Avi if he ever recalled passing by a jewelry store. "Consider the diamonds in the window," he told him. "Try and think what they look like when they come out of the mine—lumps of dirty ore. It takes a person who understands the diamond to take the shapeless mound and bring out its intrinsic beauty. That's what we do here, we look for the diamond in everyone; we help the soul's beauty come to the surface, we polish it until it gleams." Twerski looked over at Avi, his hair disheveled, hunched over, nearly hiding in his seat: "You're like that dirt-covered ore and our business is to find the diamond within and polish it until it glows."

Over the following years, Avi graduated from the treatment center, completed a stay at a halfway house, got a job in construction, and went to live in the community. One day he received a request from Annette, the manager of the halfway house he had recently left, to help unload an apartment: the family matriarch had died, and her children wanted the halfway house to have her furniture. Avi agreed to pick up the furniture and bring it over.

While carrying a sofa up the stairs, an envelope fell from between the cushions. He picked it up, and after he finished unloading the couch, he opened it. Inside was 5,000 shekel, about $1,700.

In Avi's earlier life as a burglar and drug addict, he would have broken into a house for $20. Now, he called Annette and told her about the envelope, and she said she would report it to the family.

The family was so moved by Avi's and Annette's honesty that they told her to keep the money for the halfway house, which was able to buy an additional bed, thereby providing room for an additional guest—and giving one more person the opportunity for recovery.

Avi related the story in a letter to Dr. Twerski: "When I used drugs, I would get a high for a very short time and when the high wore off I would feel terrible, worse than before. It's been three months since I found that money and every time I think about what I did, I feel good all over again. How different a feeling than a temporary fix."

A year later, Twerski recalls, "I returned to the halfway house where Avi's good deed had set off a chain of events which led to, among other things, an extra bed. There was a sign hanging above the entry. It read: DIAMONDS POLISHED HERE."[25]

PART FIVE

WHAT DO YOU DO NOW? MAKING THESE PRACTICES PART OF YOUR LIFE

CHAPTER 14

Incorporating the Principles of Ethical Speech into Daily Life

One who repeats what he has learned one hundred times cannot be compared to one who repeats it a hundred and one times.

—Babylonian Talmud, *Hagigah* 9b*

RECOVERING ALCOHOLICS KNOW that, to succeed, they can never treat liquor casually. If they attend a party where liquor is served, they avoid it, realizing that just one sip can bring about catastrophic results. If they have joined AA, they gather with others to discuss common problems of remaining sober and to give each other reinforcement. They know that just making a mental or verbal commitment to stay sober won't work; what is required is to maintain unending vigilance—and to the extent possible, to avoid being in places where alcohol will be served.

Those who would speak ethically need to be equally determined

---

* My friend David Szonyi notes: "This talmudic quote suggests that relearning something many, many times, rather than being a repetitive, and perhaps boring, intellectual experience, can lead one to a deeper and fresher understanding."

to avoid hurting others with words. They must try to refrain from becoming involved in malicious gossip and, if possible, to minimize or avoid interactions with people who engage in mean-spirited talk about others. As a rule, it is naive to think that you can spend time with such people and avoid being drawn in; at the very least, you will provide them with an audience and risk letting them unjustly lower your estimation of others. Some in the Orthodox world post a photo of the Haffetz Hayyim—who devoted great efforts to discouraging unfair speech and was the leading Jewish scholar on the laws of ethical speech—near their telephones or computers as a constant reminder to remember to speak and write fairly of others.

For most of us, the best approach to practicing ethical speech would be—to borrow from AA again—"one step at a time." What if, every day for a two-hour period, you were particularly careful to say nothing bad about anyone? Lunch or dinner might be an ideal time, since much nasty gossip is spread and analyzed at mealtimes. Of course, not all discussions about others are malicious. Good friends like to catch up about people they know in common. A good litmus test is to consider whether you are speaking about others in a way that you wouldn't mind being spoken about yourself.

Another way to begin making ethical speech a part of your life is to review periodically the principles discussed in this book. I suspect that many readers have nodded in agreement at many of the observations and anecdotes. Perhaps you've found yourself agreeing that it's wrong to disseminate negative or ugly truths about others, to spread cruel and reputation-destroying rumors, and to introduce irrelevant, embarrassing information into a quarrel. You may have finished reading sections of this book determined to refrain from ranting and raving in response to minor provocations and to desist from humiliating others.

Yet, if you're like me, it's unlikely that reading this book once will "cure" you of the tendency to use words unkindly, any more than one reading of a powerful book on the horrors of drunkenness will induce an alcoholic to become permanently sober.

For most of us, gossiping and talking to others unfairly are about as addictive as liquor is for alcoholics. Thus, if you wish to change the way you speak *about* and *to* people, you need to practice consistently the principles outlined on the following pages and, no less importantly, to be very conscious of the direction of a conversation when you are with people who don't take these principles seriously.

ON GOSSIP THAT IS TRIVIAL AND TRUE

When you make comments, even positive ones, about someone, remember how easily the conversation can drift in negative directions. A remark such as "I think Chuck is great, but there's one thing I can't stand about him," is unlikely to trigger an extended discussion of all the things about Chuck that are great; rather, the conversation probably will focus on that "one thing."

Whenever you find yourself involved in an innocuous conversation about someone but negative or intrusive comments begin to be made, remember Oliver Sipple's fate (see pages 29–30). He saved the president's life, became an overnight hero, and was the subject of many positive news stories. Yet Sipple's new status subjected him to personal scrutiny of the sort he wished to avoid and, by the time it ended, his life had been permanently and severely damaged.

Obviously, in today's world, where attitudes toward homosexuality and homosexuals have changed greatly, the impact on Sipple's life would not have been so negative—and perhaps not negative at all—but all of us have aspects of our lives that we do not want others to make known to the world. If something about us is to be made known, we want to choose when and to whom to reveal it.

NEGATIVE TRUTHS (*LASHON HA-RA*)

In probably no other area of life do so many of us regularly violate the Golden Rule as in speaking negative truths. If you entered a room and heard the people inside talking about you, what would you least like to hear them talking about? Wouldn't it be a description of your character flaws or the intimate details of your personal life? Yet when we gossip about others, those are the very things that are most likely to come up.

Is it difficult to avoid gossiping about the ugly, or just unseemly, parts of other people's lives? Definitely. It has always been, and always will be, because few things are more interesting to talk about than other people's flaws, private hurts, and scandals.

If you wish to treat others with the kindness you would have them extend to you, recall *before* you speak the advice of Jonathan Lavater from chapter 2: "Never tell evil of a man if you do not know it for a certainty, and if you know it for a certainty, then ask yourself, 'Why should I tell it?'"

Occasionally, you may have a valid reason to say something negative about another person. For example, if someone you know is considering going into business with, hiring, or dating someone you know to be inappropriate for him or her, you should tell that person—*but no one else*—what you know. When doing so, *don't* exaggerate. And if you're not certain that the information is true—but have reason to think it might be—say so: "I've heard it said that . . . but I'm not sure it's true. I don't know it as a fact, but I just think you should look into it."

Be specific about why you think this person is inappropriate. Avoid statements like, "There is a very good reason you shouldn't hire him. I can't tell you why, but believe me, don't hire him." There's always the possibility that a factor that seems disqualifying to you might not seem disqualifying to the person to whom you're speaking. But more important, this type of declaration almost always is unfair to the person about whom you're speaking. Similarly, it would be wrong to say to someone, "I don't want to have anything to do with you anymore, but I can't tell you why."

When I was a child, my father once overheard my mother reading to me the following children's rhyme:

> *I do not love you, Dr. Fell*
> *The reason why, I cannot tell,*
> *But this I know and know full well*
> *I do not love you, Dr. Fell.*

My father interrupted my mother to point out: "That's a cruel poem. The person who is speaking is being very unfair to Dr. Fell."

Remember: even when it's permissible to spread a negative truth, be specific, be precise, and be fair.

In other cases, when the negative information is no one else's business, let the words of Ben Sira, a wise citizen of ancient Israel, guide you: "Have you heard something? Let it die with you. Be strong; it will not burst you."[1]

RUMORS AND LIES (*MOTZI SHEM RA*)

Throughout history, rumors and lies have often caused as much misery as war. Over the millennia, lies about the Jews—that they caused the Black Plague by poisoning Europe's wells, that they drank the blood of non-Jews at their religious rituals, that they were involved in an international conspiracy to take over the world and enslave Gentiles—have led to the murder of millions of innocent people. Today lies told by those who claim Israel is practicing genocide against the Palestinians (whose population inside Israel has increased sevenfold since Israel's creation in 1948) are intended to help bring about the Jewish state's destruction.

Similarly, lies and rumors destroy the lives of individuals, a theme that has been poignantly addressed in literature as well as in real life. In Shakespeare's play *Othello*, Iago's fabrications cause Othello to murder Desdemona, and a twelve-year-old girl's lie, conveyed by rumormongers, prompts a woman to commit suicide in *The Children's Hour*.

Before spreading a negative report, remember the Talmud's words: "If something is as clear to you as the fact that your sister is sexually forbidden to you, [only] then say it."

And even in such a case, speak only to those who need the information. In those instances when you feel it important to pass on a rumor (for example, someone is contemplating investing funds with a person you have heard is dishonest), emphasize that your information is unconfirmed and requires further investigation.

ANGER

Dr. Solomon Schimmel, a Boston psychologist and psychotherapist, reports that he spends "more time helping clients deal with their anger than with any other emotion."[2]

Anger is a powerful and very common emotion. Yet as difficult as it is to control *what* makes us angry, we can generally control *how* we express our feelings. If you have made comments while angry that you subsequently regretted or that might have ended a relationship, observing a simple rule may well guarantee that you never do so again: *Limit the expression of your anger to the incident that provoked it.*

If you do choose to share your anger with others, avoid doing so with individuals who will inflame your feelings. Rather, choose people who are more likely to calm you and help you put things in a broader perspective.

Above all, remember that the most important person with whom you should speak is the one with whom you're angry. If your antagonist hears that you've been speaking ill of him or her to others, that individual's anger probably will grow, making reconciliation between the two of you much more difficult.

FIGHTING FAIRLY

When it comes to football, Vince Lombardi may have been right (although I think not) in the statement attributed to him: "Winning is the only thing."

But when it comes to conflicts between people, no advice could be more harmful. People who believe that winning an argument, particularly a personal one, is "the only thing" are likely to introduce unfair points into disputes and to end relationships. Remember: *Never bring in information about the person with whom you are arguing to discredit or embarrass him or her.* That's what Rabbi Yochanan did to Resh Lakish when he publicly reminded everyone witnessing their dispute that Resh Lakish once had been a thief. This nongermane and unfair information led to a permanent, tragic rupture in the two men's friendship.

Through repeated questioning of audiences over the years, I have learned that perhaps a third or more of all families have close relatives who no longer are on speaking terms. Almost invariably, the rift started with an argument that escalated, with one or both parties saying increasingly harsh things. The time to avoid making ugly comments is *before* they leave your mouth. Once they do, the other party might forgive you, but it is unlikely that he or she will forget. Would you?

HOW TO CRITICIZE

Before you criticize somebody, ask yourself three questions:

1. How do I feel about offering this criticism? Does it give me pleasure or pain?

   If part of you is looking forward to criticizing someone, hold back. Your motives are probably at least partly insincere; you may not wish to help the person so much as cut him down to size. If this is the case, he will probably respond defensively and reject your critique.

   If the thought of criticizing another pains you, yet you feel impelled to speak up, do so. Your motives probably are sincere, and your concern for the other person will shine through, making it likely that she will be able to accept, or at least hear, your criticism.

2. Does my criticism offer specific ways to change?

3. Are my words nonthreatening and reassuring?

   When criticizing, avoid the words "always" ("You're always thinking about what's good for you and don't consider anybody else's needs") and "never" ("You never think before you act"). Such words are one-dimensional and demoralize the person being criticized, and she will probably feel impelled to deny *everything* you're saying. Who would acknowledge, "Yes, it's true, I am very selfish and never think about anyone else's needs"? Rarely would a person being criticized agree that she is "really stupid" and admit that "I never think before I act."

   Be particularly careful to avoid using the words "always"

and "never" when speaking to children. In addition to hearing things more literally than adults, children have egos that tend to be especially vulnerable, and such rebukes can make them feel worthless. Keep in mind the advice of Johann Paul Friedrich to not call a child a liar but to simply "tell him that he has told a lie," so as to avoid "break[ing] down his confidence in his own character." (See the Socratic technique suggested by Dr. Isaac Herschkopf for influencing a child to tell the truth without explicitly telling the child that he or she has told a lie [pages 126–127]).

When offering criticism, think strategically: Remember the three suggestions of Moses Maimonides: "He who rebukes another . . . should

1. Administer the rebuke in private,

2. Speak to the offender gently and tenderly, and

3. Point out that he is only speaking for the wrongdoer's own good." (numerals added)

LEARNING HOW TO ACCEPT CRITICISM

Because we are capable of improving, and otherwise growing, we should regard those who criticize us *fairly* and *constructively* with the same gratitude we feel toward a physician who accurately diagnoses an ailment. Without the diagnosis, we would remain sick and likely grow sicker; without the critic's words, we might deteriorate ethically.

So when someone criticizes you, resist the temptation to point out similar or other flaws in her, which might well exist. Instead, ask yourself: *Is what she is saying true?* If her criticism seems overstated, then ask yourself another question: *Is there any validity in the criticism? Can I take what she has said and use it to improve myself?*

PUBLIC HUMILIATION

Jewish law regards humiliating another person, particularly in public, as one of the cruelest things anyone can do. Public humiliation is a trauma from which many people never fully recover, as exemplified by the seven-year-old girl whose teacher publicly ridiculed her before the whole class (pages 136–137), the overweight adolescent whose mother mocked her in front of visiting relatives and friends (pages 137–138), and the rape victim, an emergency room nurse, confronted by a criminal defense lawyer who tried to convince the jury that she was a part-time prostitute (pages 133–135).

Because public humiliation often inflicts irrevocable damage, it sometimes can be unforgivable. To avoid ever humiliating another person again, there are two things you must do:

Reflect again and again on the moral evil of shaming another person. This is particularly important for people who possess both quick tempers and sharp wits. This combination sometimes tempts them to make clever, but very hurtful, wisecracks at other people's expense. (Unfortunately, it's much harder to be clever when praising someone.) A Yiddish witticism teaches: "Who is a hero? One who suppresses a wisecrack."

When you're angry—precisely when it is hardest to exercise self-control—choose your words carefully. Even if your anger is fully justified, that only entitles you to express that anger; it does not give you the right to humiliate another person.

Once an old rabbi witnessed a young man admonishing another. Because the rebuke was tactless and very sharp, the face of the man being criticized had turned red.

The rabbi stopped the admonisher, took him aside, and informed him that he was committing a far more serious sin than had been committed by the other man.

The rebuker took offense at the rabbi's words. "What that man did was so wrong that he deserves to be humiliated, *even if it costs me my share in the World-to-Come.*"

The old rabbi later confided: "At that moment, I wondered if this young man even believed in the World-to-Come. When calm, I don't think he would have been willing to sacrifice his little finger, let alone all eternity, for the sake of delivering his rebuke. Yet, when angry, people are capable of making insane pronouncements."

Although angry people are the ones who are most likely to humiliate others, the Talmud warns us all to be careful not to do so. As noted earlier, it advises: "If somebody was hanged in a person's family, don't say to him, 'Hang up this fish for me.'" Take care that you do not let careless remarks revive painful memories for others or remind them of past humiliation.

IS LYING ALWAYS WRONG?

In interpersonal relations, truth is a very important value, but not always the highest. Although Immanuel Kant thought it preferable to let a would-be murderer kill someone rather than lie to him about the would-be victim's whereabouts, ethical common sense and love of humankind dictate that some lies are justified, not only when life is at stake but also when telling the truth would only purposelessly inflict pain. Thus, if your friend has dressed inappropriately for a social gathering and asks, "How do I look?," answer honestly. Advising him to change his clothes might be momentarily awkward, but telling him the truth will save him far greater embarrassment. But if you meet a person at a party who is inappropriately dressed and she asks you, "How do I look?," it would be pointless and cruel to say "terrible," or "totally inappropriate."

Of course, it is wrong to tell a lie when your goal is not to avoid inflicting pain, but to secure a personal advantage (the very reason so many lies are told). For example, it is wrong to make a big show of inviting someone to be your guest when you know that he will refuse, just so that he will think of you as a devoted friend. Jewish thought regards this as a form of stealing—you are "stealing" a good impression for yourself under false pretenses.

Regarding "macro" issues, lying is virtually always wrong; even when told to promote a noble cause, untruths are apt to lead to unforeseen and immoral consequences. Remember, the Allied propagandists who spread lies about German atrocities during World War I may have succeeded in strengthening anti-German feelings throughout the Allied countries. But they inadvertently helped inspire Adolf Hitler to tell his big lies both before and during World War II, while also leading others to believe that the reports of Nazi atrocities might well be mere propaganda.

Ultimately such lies are also unfortunate for those who tell them, for once people learn that they have been misled, they are less likely to believe other, perhaps true, claims made by that person.

Remember the words of Friedrich Hebbel: "One lie does not cost you one truth, but *the* truth."

NOT EVERYTHING THAT IS
THOUGHT SHOULD BE SAID

Two pieces of advice, neither of them from me:

1. "Have you heard something? Let it die with you. Be strong; it will not burst you" (Ecclesiasticus 19:10).

2. "It's so simple to be wise. Just think of something stupid to say and then don't say it" (Sam Levenson).

IF YOU ARE GOING TO GOSSIP ANYWAY, IS
IT STILL WORTH READING THIS BOOK?

Emphatically yes. The Talmud, with its realistic assessment of human nature, suggests that the large majority of people utter a "negative truth"—often a mean-spirited one—at least once daily.

Reviewing the principles of ethical speech regularly will achieve one important effect: although you may still gossip, you will do less of it. And you will probably be less unfair in discussing others.

If you do gossip, severely limit the amount of time you spend doing so, and let your comments go no further than a spouse (or a close boyfriend or girlfriend) and perhaps one or two close friends. This advice is prompted by my realistic view of human nature. The Haffetz Hayyim does, however, emphasize that unless the person to whom you are speaking needs the information, you should share it with no one.

When I suggested to an acquaintance my guidelines on limiting gossip, he responded: "But isn't it true that once you gossip at all, you're violating the principles of ethical speech, so what does it matter if you gossip a lot or a little?"

I answered: "If you tell me that you're driving on a highway tonight with a sixty-five-mile-per-hour speed limit and you plan to speed, I'll urge you to drive at seventy miles per hour rather than one hundred. At one hundred miles per hour, your violation of the law is much greater, and much worse things are likely to happen."

In short, when it comes to ethical behavior, you should make an effort to make yourself and other people better even when you know that you and they aren't going to strive for, let alone achieve, perfection.

Finally, as you try to restrain yourself from spreading a juicy bit of gossip or directing a stinging remark, remember Rabbi Harold Kushner's words: "Only God can give us credit for the angry [or other cruel] words we did not speak."[3]

WORDS THAT HEAL

Whether it be an issue of expressing gratitude, speaking to the vulnerable, using moral imagination, helping children develop a sense of self-esteem based on their goodness, or apologizing, the most important thing to remember is that words that heal must be said. Hugs, pats on the back, a warm smile, can all help, but they are not enough. The words that shaped Dr. Rachel Naomi Remen's self-image were the words *said* by her grandfather, not the kind but unsaid thoughts of her mother (see pages 174–175).

CHAPTER 15

Where Heaven and Earth Touch: A National "Speak No Evil Day"

WHAT IF WE could share our consciousness of the power of words with many others—even the whole nation?

Millions of Americans annually observe Earth Day, a day concerned with eliminating the pollution of our planet. A national "Speak No Evil Day" could work to eliminate the pollution of our emotional atmosphere, the realm in which we interact with others.

I envision Speak No Evil Day as being observed each year (on a day to be determined). I was very honored some years ago to play a role in influencing Senators Connie Mack of Florida and Joseph Lieberman of Connecticut to introduce a resolution in the U.S. Senate to establish such a day (see the appendix for the text of that resolution). Although the resolution generated much positive publicity at the time, I learned that such a resolution needed at least fifty senatorial cosponsors in order to pass. I think the time has come to renew the effort to establish a National Speak No Evil Day.

The plague of incivility has sharpened political divisions, sometimes paralyzing our government, while incivility in personal discourse and over the internet has caused people irrevocable hurt (from verbal bullying, mean-spirited gossip, and cruel outbursts of anger) and even led to suicides (from public shaming).

Speak No Evil Day would have both short- and long-term goals: to eliminate all vicious and unfair talk for twenty-four hours, and to thus plant the seed of a more permanent shift in our consciousness.

On this day, people will attempt to refrain from making a single nasty comment about others, even if true. Only in the very rare instances when it's absolutely necessary to transmit negative information will they do so. Otherwise, like those who engage in periodic cleansing fasts to purify their bodies, people will go for an entire day without uttering unfair and hurtful talk.

On this day, people also will monitor and regulate how they speak to others. Everyone will strive to keep his or her anger under control. If a person does express anger, he will do so fairly and limit his comments to the incident that provoked his ire. People likewise will argue fairly and not allow their disputes to degenerate into name-calling or other forms of verbal abuse. No one, not even a person offering deserved criticism, will humiliate another.

In short, on Speak No Evil Day, people will strive to fulfill the Golden Rule and will speak about others with the same kindness and fairness that they wish others to exercise when speaking about them.

I hope that journalists and other media professionals will be touched by the spirit of the day. While retaining the right to report *relevant* negative items about public figures, they will omit innuendos, sarcastic asides, rumors, and the publicizing of private scandals.

On Speak No Evil Day, all of us will refrain from disseminating rumors, particularly negative ones.

On this day, too, people will strive to avoid hurting and defaming groups as well as individuals. By avoiding all bigoted, intolerant, sweeping comments—even just for one day—we may finally come to view others as individuals and realize that negative stereotypes of large ethnic, religious, racial, and gender groups are very damaging, unfair, and untrue.

A rabbi once told me that his grandmother used to say, "It is not within everyone's power to be beautiful, but all of us can make sure that the words that come out of our mouths are."

Speak No Evil Day will be a twenty-four-hour period of verbal beauty:

—It will be a day when a young child who is frequently teased—or more accurately, mocked—by his classmates and called by ugly nicknames can go to school confident that no one will say a cruel word to him.

—It will be a day when an employee with a sharp-tongued boss can go to work without fearing that she will be verbally abused.

—It will be a day when that sharp-tongued boss—the type who says, "I don't get ulcers, I give them"—might come to understand how vicious such a statement is and will say nothing that will cause pain.

—It will be a day when a heavy adolescent will not have to fear a biting comment about her weight from parents or peers.

—It will be a day when a man who once served a prison sentence but who has led an exemplary life since being released will not have to fear that a journalist will publicize his earlier behavior.

—It will be a day when a congressional candidate who suffered a nervous breakdown will not have to worry that his opponent will use this painful episode to publicly humiliate him.

—It will be a day when an African American or Hispanic American can be among other Americans without fearing that she will hear prejudicial comments or ugly words about herself or her racial group.

—It will be a day when spouses who usually only complain to each other will speak instead about what they love and specifically appreciate in each other.

—It will be a day when people will use the words that heal others' emotional wounds, not those that inflict them.

In short, Speak No Evil Day will be a day when, through humankind's collective efforts, we will experience a taste of heaven on earth.

A Jewish proverb teaches: "If you will it, it is no fantasy." If we only want it enough, Speak No Evil Day is possible. Whether or not it will happen is in our hands—and mouths.

Acknowledgments for the 2019 Edition

IN ADDITION TO the people thanked in the book's earlier edition, I am very grateful to several people who helped me in the revising of *Words That Hurt, Words that Heal*. Many of these people are beloved friends and relatives, and I cannot overstate my gratitude.

Carolyn Hessel, Executive Director Emeritus of the Jewish Book Council and currently Director of the Sami Rohr Prize, honored my manuscript with two readings, catching major points while not missing minor ones. Carolyn has the rare capacity both to encourage and to criticize, and she does both brilliantly.

Dr. Isaac Herschkopf, a psychiatrist, read through the manuscript meticulously (as he has done for several of my books, most notably the two volumes of *A Code of Jewish Ethics*), and he provided both insights and valuable anecdotes on how to incorporate the principles of ethical speech into daily life.

In addition, I also profited greatly from a careful reading by Terry Wohlberg, whose perspective as a psychotherapist provided particularly helpful insights in the chapters on parents and children and on words that heal.

I also wish to thank Dr. Paul Appelbaum for clarifying for me, in his characteristically patient manner, a question concerning doctor-patient confidentiality and medical ethics.

The original version of this book was published in 1996 when my daughters Naomi and Shira were seven and five. Now, twenty-two years later, I thank them both for not only giving the book a careful reading but also assembling a great deal of material on more recent instances of the misuse of language. That they both took time off from their own very busy lives—Shira at Harvard Divinity School from her journalistic writing and Naomi from screenwriting and doctoral studies at the University of New South Wales, and teaching at the University of Canberra—was very moving to me. And I am very grateful for the many discussions I had with Ben and Tiferet and Rebecca and Rajesh about the themes of the book.

Liza Wohlberg, herself a gifted researcher and writer, stepped in near the end and provided very helpful line editing, along with both critiques and commentary.

David Wohlberg favored me with a careful reading of several chapters. On a number of occasions, his carefully and passionately worded criticisms caused me to reconsider several of my points.

Rabbi Zalman Shmotkin, director of Chabad.org, stepped in late in the process of editing and offered me some very valuable and necessary insights based particularly, but not only, on both his well-honed editorial skills and his great knowledge of the Lubavitcher Rebbe. And Reb Zalman and I were assisted by Rabbi Mendel Alperowitz, a man of wide-ranging knowledge who served as my research aide on the book *Rebbe*. It is the great good fortune of South Dakota that Reb Mendel and his wife Chaya Mushka now serve as Chabad's shluchim to that state, the last of the fifty states to establish a Chabad House.

Jake Zebede became my friend when he edited, along with HarperCollins / Harper Wave publisher Karen Rinaldi, my earlier book *Rebbe*. That Jake took the time only a few weeks after his wedding to Tania to read through large sections of this manuscript was very moving to me. And his analysis of how technology, with all its blessings, is also making people less patient and more prone to engage in personal attacks is stunningly insightful: "When we have

140 characters to disagree with someone, how much more likely are we to go for the easy target and low blows?"

On every book I have worked on over the past several decades, I have always been blessed to have editorial input from Rabbi David Woznica. Among his many strengths, David invariably manages to help me find the right way to express things that I am struggling to convey properly. On this book, I was blessed to have editorial suggestions and good advice from Beverly Woznica as well, a fount of common sense.

I would like to thank Russell Robinson, CEO of the Jewish National Fund, and Cheryl Lefland, director of the organization's Speaker's Bureau, for affording me the opportunity to speak about and develop many of these ideas at JNF events throughout the United States. JNF is today doing much extraordinary, awe-inspiring work in raising the level of Jewish life.

I would also like to acknowledge Neuriel Shore of the Jewish National Fund of Los Angeles for some very helpful input on the subject of fair speech, an issue we both care about deeply.

Howard Wiener, my neighbor and computer doctor—and one whom I am in need of often—shared with me insights from his own careful reading of the book.

Karen Wilder—typist, editor, and organizer par excellence—helped put this sometimes disorganized manuscript in perfect order with her trademark warmth, extraordinary competence, and attention to detail, and her delicious cookies.

And a thank-you to my brother-in-law Stephen Friedgood, whose sense of the aesthetic always adds beauty to our family.

A deeply felt thank-you to my friend Peter Rodriguez, whose trademark line is so consistent with the thesis of this book: "It's nice to be important, but it is even more important to be nice."

As always, I am deeply beholden to Richard Pine of Inkwell Management, my agent now for over thirty-five years. I can only repeat what I said in the original acknowledgments to this book over twenty years ago: it is difficult to find a fresh way of thanking such an extraordinary person, extraordinary friend, and extraordinary agent. And now that Eliza Rothstein, a woman of great editorial discernment and kindness, has joined Richard's team at Inkwell Management, I feel doubly blessed.

At William Morrow, my editor, Nick Amphlett, gave this book, filled with many revisions, a careful reading, and Cindy Buck made literally hundreds of improvements, which greatly improved the book's readability and clarity. I am immensely grateful.

As I look over the acknowledgments from the book's first edition, I regret to record the passing of Jean Kaplan, who, along with her late husband Dr. Bernard Kaplan, were not only beloved friends but models of the very principles discussed in this book.

In these interim years, I have lost my mother, Helen Telushkin of blessed memory, whose generosity of spirit always blessed my life, my wife Dvorah's life, and those of our children, Rebecca, Naomi, Shira, and Benjamin. Fifteen years have passed and I deeply miss her, as I do my late father, Shlomo Telushkin, and my late uncle Bernard "Bernie" Resnick, the two people of golden tongues to whom this book is dedicated. Fortunately, my beloved aunt Leonora, Bernie's wife and the most gracious person I know, remains a vibrant force in our family.

Between 2009 and 2014, I worked on *Rebbe*, a biography of Menachem Mendel Schneerson, the seventh and internationally renowned Lubavitcher Rebbe. Many of the Rebbe's teachings have penetrated and elevated me, none more than his commitment to the use of positive language (see pages 201–206). The Rebbe understood that the use of negative words impacts us in ways that most of us never think about. It is perhaps no surprise that the Chabad movement, which grew greatly under the influence of the Rebbe, has produced the most consistently optimistic movement in Jewish life—and possibly in Jewish history.

Finally, I wish to express profound gratitude to Dvorah, who has not only been hearing about the subject of this book for decades, but who stepped in, in the last weeks before I submitted the book to my publisher, and did a very careful edit. When Dvorah thinks I am making a mistake in my argument, she is not shy about expressing her viewpoint and has indeed convinced me to shift my approach on a number of occasions. In the acknowledgments to *Rebbe*, I wrote of Dvorah that "it was she who helped me cross the finish line." And once again she has done so (even bringing to my attention a whole new idea that was incorporated in the five days preceding the manuscript's submission). Dvorah is a woman of great integrity and a discerning writer and stylist. For that, and for many other reasons as well, I am blessed.

Joseph Telushkin, August 21, 2018

Acknowledgments for the Original 1996 Edition

A **NUMBER OF FRIENDS**, colleagues, and family members generously gave of their time to read drafts of this book. They provided me with critical feedback, suggestions for additional material, and, equally important, the kind of enthusiastic response that motivated me to keep working on improving it. I would like to thank Dr. Stephen Marmer, Professor David Ellenson, Dr. Antonio Wood, Rabbi Leonid Feldman, Rabbi David Woznica, Rabbi Michael Paley, Helen Telushkin, Shalva Siegel, Dr. Howard Siegel, Jeff Davidowitz, Esther Davidowitz, Cori Drasin, Kirk Douglas, and Jeff Sagansky. I am grateful as well to Lauren Janis, whose rush weekend typing efforts helped me to finally finish the manuscript, and to my friend Jonathan Mark, associate editor of *The Jewish Week*.

The chapter on "Words That Heal" was deeply influenced by the writings of, and books edited by, Rabbi Jack Riemer, a distinguished colleague who has done pathbreaking work in this area.

My wife, Dvorah, helped me refine many of my ideas during hours of discussion. She also stepped in at a point when I couldn't finish an important chapter and, with seeming effortlessness, suggested exactly what I needed to do. She was entirely correct, and it was her suggestion that enabled me, after two weeks of increasingly mounting frustration, to finish the book.

If by any chance I have inadvertently omitted someone's name, I deeply apologize.

This is the fourth book on which I have worked with David Szonyi. As always, his editorial and stylistic emendations improved my writing immensely. As I have often remarked, David is a blessing to any writer.

I am deeply grateful to Uriella Obst, whose editorial and stylistic suggestions, and the fresh perspective that she brought to the manuscript, aided me greatly in improving this book.

At William Morrow and Company, I have been blessed with two wonderful editors, Ann Bramson and Gail Kinn. Their extraordinary abilities, enthusiasm, and critical intelligence are a joyous gift to any writer. When they felt something was not working, they told me exactly what was needed, and despite my initial trepidations over some of their critiques, I usually found them to be on target. In addition, their passionate excitement about the book's message has been a continuing source of inspiration to me. I am also grateful to Elisa Petrini, who acquired the book for Morrow, and whose discussions with me of the book's ideas did so much to shape its structure. My deep thanks as well to Sonia Greenbaum, a superb copy editor.

This is the ninth book on which Richard Pine has represented me. It is difficult to find a fresh way of thanking such an extraordinary person, extraordinary friend, and extraordinary agent.

I am extremely indebted to Senators Connie Mack of Florida and Joseph Lieberman of Connecticut, and their aides Ellen Bork and Nina Bang-Jensen, for their work in sponsoring legislation to establish a nationally observed Speak No Evil Day on May 14 (the text of the senators' legislation can be found in the appendix). I was touched by their receptivity to the idea when I first met with them, and by their continual efforts to establish this day. I am deeply grateful to my friends Max and Suzanne Singer for their help.

I would also like to acknowledge my dear friends Jean and the late Dr. Bernard Kaplan of blessed memory, of Alexandria, Louisiana, two remarkable models of ethical speech and of so much else. My father, Shlomo Telushkin, and my uncle Bernie Resnick, both of blessed memory, were two of the kindest, noblest human beings I have known. My father combined within himself two traits that usually do not comfortably coexist—passionate convictions and nonjudgment toward others. He had the ability to make very different kinds of people feel totally accepted, which was a large part of his wonderful graciousness. Even during the last eighteen months of his life, when he was largely paralyzed from a stroke and often in terrible pain, he never failed to thank anyone who did the slightest favor for him. Dvorah, who met him only when he was already ill, still marvels at how appreciated and loved he made her feel.

My uncle Bernie also was a first-rate mensch. When my grandfather, Rabbi Nissen Telushkin of blessed memory, asked him as a favor to meet with a poor woman who had a legal problem—Bernie was a lawyer—he took the woman into his office right away, ahead of two clients who were waiting in his office. The woman told my grandfather with astonishment what Bernie had done. Bernie explained to my grandfather that the paying clients "would assume that a very important case had come up, which is why I was seeing this woman on such short notice, and, as a result, they wouldn't feel insulted. But if I had made this woman wait until I had dealt with all my other clients, she would have felt that I saw her as a charity case, and would have felt humiliated."

I miss them both deeply, and feel privileged to be able to dedicate this book in their honor.

Appendix:

Text of Senate Resolution to Establish a National "Speak No Evil Day"

On July 17, 1995, Senator Connie Mack of Florida submitted, on behalf of himself and Senator Joseph Lieberman of Connecticut, the following resolution to the first session of the 104th Congress:

RESOLUTION
To designate May 16, 1996, and May 14, 1997, as "National Speak No Evil Day," and for other purposes.

Whereas words used unfairly, whether expressed through excessive anger, unfair criticism, public and private humiliation, bigoted comments, cruel jokes, or rumors and malicious gossip, traumatize and destroy many lives;

Whereas an unwillingness or inability of many parents to control what they say when angry causes the infliction of often irrevocably damaging verbal abuse on their children;

Whereas bigoted words are often used to dehumanize entire religious, racial, and ethnic groups, and inflame hostility in a manner that may lead to physical attacks;

Whereas the spreading of negative, often unfair, untrue or

exaggerated, comments or rumors about others often inflicts irrevocable damage on the victim of the gossip, the damage epitomized in the expression "character assassination";

Whereas the inability of a person to refrain for 24 hours from speaking unkind and cruel words demonstrates a lack of control as striking as the inability of an alcoholic to refrain for 24 hours from drinking liquor; Now therefore, be it

Resolved, That the Senate designates May 14, 1996, and May 14, 1997, as "National Speak No Evil Day." The Senate requests that the President issue a proclamation calling on the people of the United States to observe the days with appropriate ceremonies and activities, including educational endeavors.

Notes

Introduction: The Twenty-Four-Hour Test

1. Jewish law labels such speech *ona'at dvarim*, "wronging with words," and regards it as a serious offense.

2. The early twentieth-century poem "Incident" by the African American poet Countee Cullen provides a powerful poetic depiction of the power of words to hurt:

    Once riding in old Baltimore,
    Heart-filled, head-filled with glee
    I saw a Baltimorean
    Keep looking straight at me.

    Now I was eight and very small
    And he was no whit bigger,
    And so I smiled, but he poked out
    His tongue, and called me, "Nigger."

    I saw the whole of Baltimore
    From May until December;
    Of all the things that happened there
    That's all that I remember.

3. *Midrash Psalms* 120. I am following—with minor changes—the translation cited in Earl Schwartz, *Moral Development: A Practical Guide for Jewish Teachers* (Denver: Alternatives in Religious Education Publications, 1983), 78. This book contains a particularly valuable chapter (71–82) on how to teach children to refrain from gossiping, slandering, and shaming others.

4. Cited in Stephen R. Covey and David Hatch, *Everyday Greatness* (Nashville: Thomas Nelson, 2009), 176.

Chapter 1: The (Insufficiently Recognized) Power of Words to Hurt

1. Throughout history, words have proven father to the deed. The Nazis and their collaborators would have been unlikely to succeed in carrying out the

Holocaust were it not for the centuries-long legacy of anti-Jewish words, expressions, and writings that they inherited. Among those were *The Protocols of the Elders of Zion*; the expression popularized in 1879 by the German historian Heinrich von Treitschke, "The Jews are our misfortune," which became the Nazis' slogan; and of course, the infamous term "Christ-killer" itself is a legacy of Christian antisemitism.

2. Rush Limbaugh, *The Ways Things Ought to Be* (New York: Pocket Books, 1992), 194, 204.

3. Cited in Dennis Prager, "Liberals and the Decline of Dialogue," *Ultimate Issues* (January/March 1990), 11.

4. Cited in Ethan Bronner, *Battle for Justice: How the Bork Nomination Shook America* (New York: W. W. Norton, 1982), 98. See the discussion of the attacks on Bork in Stephen Carter, *The Confirmation Mess* (New York: Basic Books, 1994), 45–50. Carter, a law professor at Yale and himself a liberal, writes: "It is plain that the campaign to defeat [Bork] lifted snippets of his scholarship and his judicial decisions very far out of their contexts, distorting or misleading to raise popular ire" (45). As regards the senator's attack on Bork, Carter writes that it "was surely beyond the pale" (50).

5. In the aftermath of this congressman's remark, the National Jewish Democratic Council issued a statement that "invoking the Holocaust to make a political point is never acceptable." As a general rule, I have found that "watch your words" and "think before you speak" are two expressions that are often—way too often—ignored. In the 2016 political campaign, Democratic candidate Hillary Clinton was asked at the first debate among the Democratic candidates, "You've all made a few people upset over your political careers. Which enemy are you most proud of?" Hillary Clinton responded by first reeling off some of her expected foes, the NRA (National Rifle Association), the health insurance companies, and the drug companies. Clinton then said, "The Iranians. Probably the Republicans." She laughed when she said "the Republicans," but obviously her comment was not really a joke. (She made these remarks many months before Trump's campaign repeatedly made personal attacks against her.) For a person seeking the Democratic Party's presidential nomination, to say that she was more proud to be hated by the Republicans than by Iran—a country whose leadership has long denounced America as "the great Satan" and that organizes demonstrations at which tens of thousands of people shout "Death to America," a country that sponsors terrorism throughout the world and is committed to securing an atom bomb and dropping it on Israel—causes a substantial part of the country, Republicans, to feel that she has just declared herself to be *their* enemy. Joe Biden, the Democratic vice president, was deeply upset by Clinton's comment: "I don't consider Republicans enemies. They're friends."

6. Cited in Michael Medved, *Hollywood vs. America* (New York: HarperCollins/Zondervan, 1992), 194.

7. Marian Wright Edelman, *Guide My Feet: Prayers and Meditation on Loving and Working for Children* (Boston: Beacon Press, 1995), xxiv–xxv.
8. Medved, *Hollywood vs. America*, 150, 193.
9. Medved, *Hollywood vs. America*, 150.
10. Eminem's obsession with violence is directed against not only women but also gays ("That I'll still be able to break a motherfu . . . table, / over the back of a couple of faggots and break it in half"), and even against his own mother, for whom he expressed the wish that she "burn in hell." (I am happy to report that Eminem did subsequently apologize for that song, "Cleanin' out My Closet.")

Chapter 2: The Irrevocable Damage Inflicted by Gossip

1. Babylonian Talmud, *Berachot* 58a.
2. Stephen Bates, *If No News, Send Rumors: Anecdotes of American Journalism* (New York: Henry Holt, 1989), 142–143. I am omitting the name of the reporter who originally publicized the information in the *Los Angeles Times*. Sipple's brother has noted that years later there was a reconciliation.
3. American law, it should be noted, does protect citizens from invasion of privacy. Thus, a newspaper is forbidden to pick out a name at random from a telephone book and assign reporters to write an exposé about the person. Arguing that the reporters had invaded his privacy, Sipple sued the newspapers. The suit was eventually dismissed on the grounds that by intervening to save the president's life, Sipple had in essence become a public figure; hence, he no longer was exempt from having his privacy invaded. How apt seems the cynical proverb "No good deed goes unpunished."
4. For examples of what constitutes such "dust," see pages 32–33.
5. Despite Churchill's vigorous denial, one still finds this nasty quip commonly attributed to him in anthologies, providing yet another example of how impossible it is to recover all the feathers once they've been scattered to the wind.
6. Ed Koch, *Citizen Koch: An Autobiography* (New York: St. Martin's Press, 1992), 248–249.
7. Bret Stephens, "When the White House Lies About You," *New York Times*, July 28, 2017.
8. Bob Woodward, *Washington Post*, March 2, 1989.
9. Quoted in Larry Sabato, *Feeding Frenzy: How Attack Journalism Has Transformed American Politics* (New York: Free Press, 1991), 181.
10. A short, insightful overview and discussion of the Tower episode can be found in Adrian Havill, *Deep Truth: The Lives of Bob Woodward and Carl Bernstein* (New York: Carol Publishing, 1993), 209.
11. Babylonian Talmud, *Shabbat* 145b.
12. *USA Today*, May 18, 1994, 1.
13. Indeed, the victim often wishes that he or she were dead. New York's former mayor Ed Koch devoted a lifetime to creating an image of himself as an idealistic and honest, if somewhat ornery, civil servant. Yet during his third

term, a number of reporters exposed several instances of Koch's appointees acting dishonestly. When some suggested that the illegalities reached into the mayor's office as well, Koch was thrown into a profound depression. In his memoir, *Citizen Koch*, he reports that although he knew he wasn't a thief, he realized that many people who read the articles would conclude otherwise: "My integrity was the most important thing to me; *my good name meant more to me than anything else I had* . . . , I never minded if people disliked me for the positions I took, or for the things I said, but I simply could not accept that people might think I was dishonest. . . . It was a very painful time. There were even moments when I thought seriously of killing myself I really did. I thought about it in tactical terms, and I thought about it in spiritual terms. . . . If only I had a gun. Thank God I had convinced Bob McGuire [the police commissioner] to remove the gun from my bathroom safe all those years ago. If I had had it, at that vulnerable point, I really think I might have used it. A gun would have done the job nicely, cleanly, quickly. I think it's entirely possible that if I had a gun nearby, in the spring and summer of 1986, I would not be here today . . . in my weakest moment, I might have just determined to get the whole ordeal over with" (emphasis added; 212–214).

Although he overcame the impulse to kill himself, Koch is convinced that the anxiety generated by the malicious attacks on his character contributed significantly to his 1987 stroke. Fortunately, it eventually became clear that the mayor had engaged in no dishonest activities and his good name was restored. But at what cost!

14. An account of Seigenthaler's nightmarish episode can be found in Daniel Solove, *The Future of Reputation: Gossip, Rumor, and Privacy on the Internet* (New Haven: Yale University Press, 2007), 142–144. The one good to emerge from this story is that Wikipedia changed its policy and now requires writers to register before creating new articles.

15. Hellman did not use fiction to create a wildly exaggerated morality tale on the perils of a vicious tongue. Rather, she based her story on a similar event in Edinburgh in 1809, chronicled by the British writer William Roughead in his 1930 book *Bad Companions*.

16. I read this somewhere, but unfortunately don't remember who said it. I would appreciate a reader sending me information as to the author of this statement.

Chapter 3: The Lure of Gossip

1. Ironically, Shakespeare put this highly sensitive and insightful comment in the mouth of Iago, the villain of *Othello*.

2. Occasionally, there could be a financial motive for spreading gossip, as when a business owner disseminates stories about a competitor with the hope of driving him or her out of business.

3. Another possible reason for the intense curiosity about the royal couple: Diana's predicament reminded both adults and children of childhood fairy

tales about unhappy princesses, and millions of men undoubtedly fanta-sized that they could inspire in Diana the love her royal husband could not.

4. Samuel Warren and Louis Brandeis, "The Right to Privacy," *Harvard Law Review*, December 15, 1890, reprinted in Tom Goldstein, ed., *Killing the Messenger: 100 Years of Media Criticism* (New York: Columbia University Press, 1989), 9.

5. Deborah Tannen, *You Just Don't Understand: Women and Men in Conversation* (New York: William Morrow, 1990), 107.

6. Alan Dershowitz, *Chutzpah* (Boston: Little, Brown, 1991), 15. I wonder if Dershowitz is correct in his assumption that the gossipmonger was truly re-lieved to learn that so prominent a Jew had not intermarried; if nothing else, such knowledge deprived her of a juicy bit of gossip. On the other hand, the fact that she could now tell an anecdote recounting her "friendship" and conversation with Mrs. Dershowitz, mother of the well-known professor and attorney, might have been sufficient compensation for no longer being able to spread an untrue bit of gossip.

7. Jack Levin and Arnold Arluke, *Gossip: The Inside Scoop* (New York: Plenum Press, 1987), 14–16. Levin and Arluke undertook no further study of the personalities or motives of the respondents who claimed to have attended a wedding that never occurred. But they cite another study of people who spread false gossip, albeit unknowingly. The social psychologists Ralph Rosnow and Gary Fine investigated the 1969 rumor, spread largely on col-lege campuses, that Beatles star Paul McCartney had died and the Beatles were keeping his death a secret. They discovered that the people who ini-tially circulated this story generally were less popular, dated less often, and had fewer friends than those who rejected the rumor and/or didn't spread it. As Levin and Arluke summarize the study's conclusion: "Because gossip of-ten places people at the center of attention, it also, at least temporarily, en-hances their status with others. This may explain why gossipmongers come from the most isolated, least popular members of a group. After all, they are the ones who most need something to make them socially acceptable" (16). For the Rosnow and Fine study, see Ralph Rosnow and Gary Fine, "Inside Rumors," *Human Behavior* (1974), 64–68.

8. Babylonian Talmud, *Bava Bathra* 164b. The first view expressed in the Tal-mud is that every person speaks negative truths (*lashon ha-ra*) every day. When this view is challenged, the Rabbis say that, at the very least, every person speaks "the dust of *lashon ha-ra*" (*avak lashon ha-ra*) daily.

Chapter 4: Is It Ever Appropriate to Reveal Humiliating or Harmful Information About Another?

1. Haffetz Hayyim, *Shmirat ha-Lashon* [Guarding One's Tongue] 4:1. I have followed, with minor variations, Rabbi Alfred Cohen's translation in "Pri-vacy: A Jewish Perspective," in *Halacha and Contemporary Society*, ed. Alfred S. Cohen (New York: KTAV, 1984), 234–235.

2. Cohen, "Privacy," 213–218.
3. Rabbi Cohen's ruling is based on the broad application that Jewish law gives to the biblical verse "Do not stand by while your neighbor's blood is shed" (Leviticus 19:16); see page 65.
4. Rabbi Alfred S. Cohen, "On Maintaining a Professional Confidence," *Journal of Halacha and Contemporary Society* 7 (Spring 1984): 73–87; 5, 78.
5. A broad outline of the Tarasoff case, and the various justices' opinions, can be found in "Tarasoff vs. the Regents of the University of California et al.," in *Today's Moral Problems*, 3rd ed., ed. Richard A. Wasserstrom (New York: Macmillan, 1985), 243–262. The reasoning of Justice Matthew Tobriner, ruling for the majority, strikes me as morally just: "The risk that unnecessary warnings be given is a reasonable price to pay for the lives of possible victims that may be saved. We would hesitate to hold that the therapist who is aware that his patient expects to attempt to assassinate the president of the United States would not be obligated to warn the authorities because the therapist cannot predict with accuracy that his patient will commit the crime."
6. It seems to me that had the two doctors followed this proposed guideline, there is a good chance that Tatiana Tarasoff would not have been murdered. Undoubtedly, if Poddar had confided to his psychologist his intent to kill the psychologist's family members, the doctor would have warned them against Poddar. And had the psychologist in such a case requested his supervisor's advice, I doubt that his supervisor would have instructed him not to reveal the threats to anyone, including his family members.
7. At the end of the film, a jury finds the priest not guilty, although the whole town assumes that he is. The murderer's wife, shocked at the townspeople's cruelty toward the priest, blurts out that she knows him to be innocent. At this point, her husband murders her, and the priest's reputation is saved. Unfortunately, by then the cost in both innocent life and ruined reputations has been very great.
8. In an indirect reference to the secrecy of the confessional, the murderer says to the priest, Father Koesler, "I had to tell someone. Somebody who couldn't tell anybody else." See William X. Kienzle, *The Rosary Murders* (New York: Random House, 1985), 175. Father Koesler feels compelled to solve the crime himself, but without utilizing any of the information he gained during confession. Unfortunately, more innocent people are murdered before he succeeds, and those deaths probably would have been averted had the priest revealed what he learned during confession.
9. Kienzle, *The Rosary Murders*, 176.

Chapter 5: Privacy and Public Figures

1. Stephen Bates, *If No News, Send Rumors: Anecdotes of American Journalism* (New York: Henry Holt, 1989), 150. Bates's book is a fascinating collection of several hundred anecdotes, many of them detailing instances of irresponsible and immoral journalism.

2. David Nyberg, *The Varnished Truth: Truth Telling and Deceiving in Ordinary Life* (Chicago: University of Chicago Press, 1992), 129.

3. Larry Sabato's *Feeding Frenzy: How Attack Journalism Has Transformed American Politics* (New York: Free Press, 1991), a study of the impact of what the author calls "attack journalism" on American political life, cites thirty-six years of Gallup poll samplings of Americans' opinions of the Democratic and Republican presidential candidates. One question measures the combined rate of respondents' "very favorable" impressions of the nominees (2016 data cited in the *Washington Post*, March 3, 2017):

    1952—84%
    1956—94%
    1960—77%
    1964—76%
    1968—63%
    1972—63%
    1976—69%
    1980—51%
    1984—68%
    1988—42%
    2016—36%

    Sabato notes that while it is true that many of the unfortunate events that occurred during the late 1960s and 1970s were precisely the sort that provoke cynicism (the Vietnam War, Watergate, the Iran hostage crisis), "this period of growing cynicism coincides almost precisely with the new era of freewheeling 'anything goes' journalism" (207–208).

    As an example of journalistic excess, the media analyst Stephen Bates (*If No News, Send Rumors*, 124) reports that in 1987 "*The New York Times* asked each presidential candidate for copies of medical and psychiatric records, school records (including high school grades), birth certificates, marriage and driver's licenses, employment records, financial statements, tax returns, and lists of closest friends . . . it [also] asked the candidates to waive their rights of privacy to any confidential files the FBI and CIA kept on them." At the time, the *Chicago Tribune* columnist Mike Royko called a *Times* spokesperson and asked her to supply similar information about the newspaper's editor. She hung up on him. The *Times* subsequently backed off from its demand for FBI and CIA files and for medical records unrelated to "fitness for the presidency."

4. Sabato, *Feeding Frenzy*, 207–208. Many examples in this chapter are taken from this extraordinarily thorough and thoughtful study of the impact of intrusive journalism on American life.

5. Quoted in Sabato, *Feeding Frenzy*, 208.

6. In a 1973 article summarizing Supreme Court decisions for the year, the *New York Times* omitted any mention of one: "The Justices had announced,"

Bates notes, "that they would not revive a paternity suit in which the defendant was the *Times* publisher." Bates, *If No News, Send Rumors*, 54–55.

7. Quoted in Sabato, *Feeding Frenzy*, 212.

Chapter 6: Controlling Rage and Anger

1. For this insight into the nature of Moses's sin, I am indebted to my friend, and a great Bible scholar, the late Professor Jacob Milgrom.

2. Michael Caine, *Acting in Film* (New York: Applause Theater Book Publishers, 1990), 115–117. Caine, whose book reveals him to be a person of considerable ethical sensitivity, offers a useful and reliable guideline for anyone whose bad temper can cause him or her to say unfair things: "Never, ever, under any circumstance, shout at anybody who is lower on the ladder than you are." In other words, don't scream at anybody who doesn't have the right to shout back. As Caine explains, to do so is to take "a monstrously unfair advantage" (117).

3. Gelles convincingly speculates that some people get drunk "knowing their inebriation will give them an excuse for violence." He probably doesn't mean physical violence alone. In Edward Albee's brilliant play *Who's Afraid of Virginia Woolf?* a couple get drunk, in large measure, it would appear, to allow themselves to say the most vicious things to each other, all the while knowing that they have a readily available excuse the next morning, something along the lines of "I'm really sorry, but don't hold me responsible for things I say when I'm drunk." Whether one spouse will hold the other responsible eventually becomes irrelevant, since the abuse will have wreaked its damage. For just as each would not have fallen in love had their partner acted with such rage during their courtship, so too their love won't endure if the spouses refuse to curb their anger.

4. I am indebted to Rabbi Zelig Pliskin for this commonsensical proof that we have far more power to control our anger than many of us are willing to admit.

5. Moses Maimonides, "The Laws of Personality Development," *Mishneh Torah* 1:4.

6. Some modern scholars note that Seneca wasn't really advocating such total passivity. Professor Solomon Schimmel, who discusses this passage in *The Seven Deadly Sins* (88ff.), argues that the reason for Harpagus's response was not indifference to his children's deaths: he feared, rather, being invited to eat more of his children's flesh. According to Schimmel, "Seneca only wants to demonstrate that we have the capacity to conceal even intense anger. Actually, he felt that a more honorable response for Harpagus . . . would have been to commit suicide rather than flatter monstrous kings" (252, n. 7). The citation from Seneca himself can be found in his chapter "On Anger," sects. 291–293.

7. Moses Maimonides, "The Laws of Personality Development," *Mishneh Torah* 1:4.

8. Aristotle, "The Virtue Concerned with Anger," *The Nicomachean Ethics*, 4:5.

9. Rabbi Abraham Joshua Heschel comments on this passage: "Anger and mercy are not opposites" (*The Prophets*, 283). Or rather, they need not be opposites. While anger devoid of compassion might be an appropriate response to a Hitler, a Stalin, or a suicide bomber, in the overwhelming majority of instances the demonizing of the person at whom we are angry will lead us to act in a manner we will come to regret.

10. See the discussion of Maimonides's and Aristotle's attitudes on anger in Joseph Telushkin, *A Code of Jewish Ethics*, vol. 1, *You Shall Be Holy* (New York: Bell Tower / Crown Publishing, 2006), 259–261.

11. Carol Tavris, *Anger* (New York: Touchstone, 1989), 152 (emphasis added).

Chapter 7: Fighting Fairly

1. Babylonian Talmud, *Bava Mezia* 84a.

2. The story also contains a great puzzle. Although Rabbi Yochanan was Resh Lakish's teacher and the greater sage, it was his behavior, not Resh Lakish's, that seems more worthy of censure. After all, it was he who, by mocking Resh Lakish's background as a gladiator and a thief, turned an intellectual argument into a personal attack. To do so was not only cruel (Jewish law considers it a serious sin to remind a penitent of his earlier misdeeds [Babylonian Talmud, *Bava Mezia* 58b]) but also in no way advanced Rabbi Yochanan's position. Thus, Resh Lakish's pained, sarcastic response has always struck me as understandable, even reasonable. Yet the Talmud seems to suggest that because Resh Lakish's comment hurt Rabbi Yochanan's feelings, he was afflicted with a mortal illness. His sickness and death seem so unjust, however, that I am moved to suggest a more "naturalistic" explanation. Resh Lakish had become religious solely because of Rabbi Yochanan's influence. Thus, when his teacher humiliated him in public, Resh Lakish became so despondent that he lost the will to live. We know that great emotional stress suppresses the immune system and leaves the body extremely vulnerable to serious illness. Resh Lakish's illness paralleled Rabbi Yochanan's subsequent collapse; in both cases, extreme mental depression led to a sharp physical decline, and eventually death.

3. *Ethics of the Fathers* 2:10.

Chapter 8: How to Criticize and How to Accept Rebuke

1. Isaac Asimov, *I, Asimov: A Memoir* (New York: Doubleday, 1994), 49.

2. Asimov, *I, Asimov*, 51.

3. Asimov, *I, Asimov*, 52.

4. Asimov, *I, Asimov*, 50.

5. *Genesis Rabbah* 54:3.

6. The tone of a caring critic is precisely what was lacking in N.'s encounters with Asimov; the teacher's undisguised hostility hurt the young writer as much as his words.

7. Moses Maimonides, "The Laws of Personality Development," *Hilkhot De'ot* 6:7.

8. It's hard to know what motivated N. In the first instance, perhaps he believed that dismissing Asimov's writing with a four-letter word would ingratiate him with his other students. But when he offered his private criticism, his motive was probably sadistic. He clearly resented having to include in the school's journal a story he didn't like. Because he derived no pleasure from publishing the story, he wanted to ensure that Asimov had none either. Whatever justification there might be for N.'s first criticism—though crudely offered, it was presumably intended to help Asimov develop his writing skills—there is none for his second gratuitously dismissive attack.

9. Cited in Zelig Pliskin, *Love Your Neighbor* (Jerusalem: Aish HaTorah Publications, 1997), 287–288.

10. Babylonian Talmud, *Yevamot* 65b.

11. Rabbi Shlomo Yosef Zevin, *A Treasury of Chassidic Tales on the Torah* (Jerusalem and New York: Mesorah Publications / Hillel Press, 1980), 189–191. I have based this excerpt on Uri Kaploun's translation of Rabbi Zevin's rendering of the tale.

12. Babylonian Talmud, *Arakhin* 16b.

13. Rabbi Kook offered two other reasons as well: "He never once told me of anything said by my fierce opponents, who were continually denigrating and defaming me, and whenever he asked a favor of me, it was never for himself but only for others." See Simcha Raz, *A Tzaddik in Our Time* (Jerusalem and New York: Feldheim, 1976), 85–86.

14. Dov Katz, *T'nuat Ha-Mussar* [The Mussar Movement], 5 vols. (Tel Aviv: 1945–1952), 1:315–316.

Chapter 9: Between Parents and Children

1. Babylonian Talmud, *Ta'anit* 20a–b.

2. Miriam Adahan, *Raising Children to Care: A Jewish Guide to Childrearing* (Spring Valley, NY: Feldheim, 1988), 161.

3. Cited in Doris Kearns Goodwin, *No Ordinary Time: Franklin and Eleanor Roosevelt: The Home Front in World War II* (New York: Simon & Schuster, 1994), 93. The effect of Eleanor's mother's disapproving, unloving attitude was so profound that when her mother died a month after Eleanor's eighth birthday, "Death meant nothing to me, and one fact wiped out everything else—my father [who had been away for a long time would be] back, and I would see him very soon" (94).

4. Babylonian Talmud, *Bava Kamma* 86a–b.

5. Maimonides, "Law of Character Development," 6:8.

6. Rabbi Abraham Twerski, M.D., and Ursula Schwartz, Ph.D., *Positive Parenting: Developing Your Child's Potential* (Brooklyn, NY: ArtScroll/Mesorah, 1996), 223.

7. Gottfried R. von Kronenberger, *Signs of the Times* (Boise, ID: Southern Pub. Assoc., 1989).
8. Babylonian Talmud, *Shabbat* 10b.
9. Lewis Grizzard, *My Daddy Was a Pistol, and I'm a Son of a Gun* (New York: Dell, 1986), 11.

Chapter 10: The Cost of Public Humiliation

1. Babylonian Talmud, *Bava Mezia* 58b.
2. Babylonian Talmud, *Bava Mezia* 58b, and Maimonides, "Laws of Character Development," *Mishneh Torah* 6:8. See also Telushkin, *You Shall Be Holy*, 285–287.
3. The incident concerning the $500,000 donation is recounted in Bates, *If No News, Send Rumors*, 142. I very much hope that in citing this anecdote and others, I have not further embarrassed the individuals involved, and I apologize if I have done so. However, it is very difficult, if not impossible, to make people aware of how terrible it is to shame another person in public without citing specific instances. I have tried to cite only cases that already have been widely publicized or whose participants' identities can be concealed.

   In *Scandal: The Culture of Mistrust in American Politics* (New York: Times Books, 1991), Suzanne Garment reports the case of a highly regarded lawyer, a former president of the American Bar Association, who was offered the post of deputy attorney general in the Reagan administration in April 1988. The day after he was nominated, the *St. Louis Post-Dispatch* published a story about him that contained the charge by an ex-bookkeeper in his law firm that he had had an affair with her. In fact, the ex-bookkeeper had embezzled $147,000 from the firm and had claimed at her recently concluded trial that the lawyer had allowed her to steal the money because of their relationship. The jury rejected this rather implausible defense and convicted her. The *Post-Dispatch* reported that the ex-bookkeeper, who had not yet been sentenced, now wanted to testify at the lawyer's confirmation hearings. Within days, her charges, which were totally without foundation, were being headlined in other parts of the country (for example, on page 1 of the *New York Daily News*). Two weeks later, the newspaper noted that its reporters had investigated the ex-bookkeeper intensively and found that nearly every significant detail she provided about her background had been proven false. From the perspective of ethics, this investigation should have been conducted *before* the article containing her defamation of the nominee appeared. By the time the newspaper's "correction" was made, the man had withdrawn as a nominee, citing the intolerable pressures on himself and his family. Ten days later, the judge who sentenced the ex-bookkeeper called her a "pathological liar" (289–290).
4. Babylonian Talmud, *Bava Mezia* 58b.
5. Sabato, *Feeding Frenzy*, 161; for Atwater's apology to Turnipseed, see 271, note 65. Unfortunately, the evil generated when one person publicly humili-

ates another often grows with time. In 1988, Turnipseed, still nurturing a grudge against Atwater, helped spread an untrue rumor of adultery against Republican vice presidential candidate Dan Quayle (although Turnipseed apparently thought it was true). Turnipseed's grievance was almost certainly not against Quayle but against his campaign manager, Lee Atwater (161).

6. Eleanor Randolph, "The Political Legacy of Baaad Boy Atwater," *New York Times*, September 19, 2008.

7. Atwater also apologized to Michael Dukakis, the Democratic presidential candidate in 1988, for the mean-spirited campaign Atwater had managed on behalf of George H. W. Bush. In the last months of his life, Atwater also summoned up another recollection: "After the [1988] election, when I would run into Ron Brown [head of the Democratic National Committee], I would say hello and then pass him off to one of my aides. I actually thought that talking to him would make me appear vulnerable. [Now], since my illness, Ron has been enormously kind. . . . He writes and calls regularly—and I have learned a lesson. Politics and human relations are separate. I may disagree with Ron Brown's message, but I can love him as a man." Tom Turnipseed, "What Lee Atwater Learned," *Washington Post*, April 16, 1991.

8. Seymour Wishman's abusive cross-examination of the complainant in the rape case and his subsequent pangs of guilt are discussed in his *Confessions of a Criminal Lawyer* (New York: Viking Penguin, 1982), 3–18. According to Wishman, the justification "I was only doing my job," which criminal lawyers often offer for their brutal behavior and for getting people acquitted who will go on to commit more violent crimes, was starting to sound like a Nazi affirmation. He does go on to note, however, that "I still believed our legal system was better than any other I know of" (151).

9. George Bernard Shaw, *Saint Joan* (New York: Viking Penguin, 1951), 154.

10. Merle Miller, *Plain Speaking: An Oral Biography of Harry S. Truman* (New York: Berkley Publishing, 1974), 401–402.

11. Miller, *Plain Speaking*, 401–402.

12. Cited in Rabbenu Bachya, *Encyclopedia of Torah Thoughts*, translated and annotated by Rabbi Dr. Charles B. Chavel (New York: Shilo Press, 1980), 210. Rabbenu Bachya attributes this teaching to a book called *Ma'asei Torah*, written by the third-century Rabbi Judah the Prince; recent scholarly investigations suggest, however, that *Ma'asei Torah* was composed several hundred years later.

13. Robert Wilson, ed., *Character Above All* (New York: Simon & Schuster, 1996), 61. In addition to his sensitivity about not humiliating people, Eisenhower displayed a commonsense intellect that was often underestimated within the academic and intellectual communities. In a 1945 letter that Eisenhower wrote to Chief of Staff George Marshall immediately after visiting the Nazi concentration camp at Ohrdruf, Germany, he commented: "The visual

evidence . . . of starvation and cruelty was so overwhelming as to leave me a bit sick. In one room, where there were piled up twenty or thirty naked men, killed by starvation, General Patton would not even enter. He said he would get sick if he did so. I made the visit deliberately, in order to be in a position to give firsthand evidence of these things if ever, in the future, there develops a tendency to charge these allegations merely to 'propaganda.'" Compare Eisenhower's prescient comment, intuited as early as 1945, that forces would arise to deny the Holocaust with the record of Professor Noam Chomsky, the highly acclaimed MIT linguist and anti-Israel, anti-American, left-wing polemicist. Chomsky has aggressively defended the right of Robert Faurisson, a French university professor, to teach that the Holocaust never happened. When Herbert Mitgang of the *New York Times* asked Chomsky to comment on the professor's views, Chomsky noted that he had no views that he wished to state, prompting the longtime *New Republic* editor Martin Peretz to comment, "On the question, that is, as to whether or not six million Jews were murdered, Noam Chomsky apparently is an agnostic." I assume Chomsky does believe the Holocaust occurred, but his passionate espousal of Faurisson's right to deny it, coupled with comparisons he has often drawn between Israel and the Nazis, reflects poorly on his character and common sense.

14. Babylonian Talmud, *Bava Mezia* 59b.

Chapter 11: Is Lying Always Wrong?

1. Babylonian Talmud, *Ketubot* 16b–17a.
2. "On Lying," in *Treatises on Various Subjects*, ed. R. J. Deferrari, vol. 14 (New York: Catholic University of American Press, 1952), 66. Responding to Augustine's prohibition, Catholic tradition introduced the concept of the "mental reservation." For example, if a feverish patient asks a doctor what his temperature is, the physician is permitted to answer, "Your temperature is normal today," while making the "mental reservation" that a high temperature is normal for someone in the patient's physical condition. Charles McFadden, *Medical Ethics*, cited in Sissela Bok, *Lying: Moral Choice in Public and Private Life* (New York: Vintage Books, 1989).

   Among Saint Augustine's most devoted admirers was John Henry Cardinal Newman, perhaps the nineteenth century's best-known convert to Catholicism and one of the century's renowned Catholic theologians. In his book *Anglican Difficulties*, Newman argued against all lies in terms even more forceful than those used by Augustine: "The Catholic Church holds it better for the sun and moon to drop from heaven, for the earth to fail, and for all the many millions who are upon it to die of starvation in extremist agony . . . than that one soul . . . should commit one venial sin, should tell one willful untruth, though it harmed no one."
3. Quoted in Michael Berenbaum, *The World Must Know* (Boston: Little, Brown, 1993), 169.

4. Immanuel Kant, "On a Supposed Right to Lie from Benevolent Motives," in *The Critique of Practical Reason*, ed. and trans. Lewis White Beck (Chicago: University of Chicago Press, 1994), 346–350.

5. Bok, *Lying*, 44. The kind of potentially lethal commitment to truth espoused by Kant prompted Thomas Jefferson to note in a letter to a friend: "State a moral case to a ploughman and a professor. The former will decide it as well, and often better than the latter, because he has not been led astray by artificial rules." Quoted in Nyberg, *The Varnished Truth*, 205–206.

6. Babylonian Talmud, *Yevamot* 63a, based on Jeremiah 9:4.

7. Babylonian Talmud, *Sukkah* 46b.

8. Babylonian Talmud, *Hullin* 94a.

9. Babylonian Talmud, *Hullin* 94a.

10. Babylonian Talmud, *Yevamot* 65b.

11. Somerset Maugham, *A Writer's Notebook* (New York: Penguin Books, 1993), 286.

12. Graham Greene, *The Heart of the Matter* (New York: Viking, 1948), 59.

13. Norman Cohn, *Warrant for Genocide* (New York: Harper & Row, 1966).

14. Despite his mid-twentieth-century reputation as one of the world's greatest historians, Toynbee seems to have possessed a strangely limited commitment to telling the truth. In his later years, he compared Zionism to Nazism in *Study of History* (New York: Oxford University Press, 1947–1957), going so far as to argue that, "on the Day of Judgment, the gravest crime standing to the German Nationalists' account might be, not that they had exterminated a majority of Western Jews, but that they had caused the surviving remnant of Jewry to stumble [and perform Nazi-like acts against the Arabs of Palestine]" (8:290n). In volume 12 of his *Study of History* (*Reconsiderations*), he wrote: "In the Jewish Zionists I see disciples of the Nazis" (627–628). Whatever one's position vis-à-vis the Arab-Israel conflict, it is a lie to argue that any symmetry exists between the Nazis' behavior toward the Jews and the Jews' toward the Palestinians. Toynbee had every right to oppose Zionism; he had no right to lie about it. As the late Senator Daniel Patrick Moynihan put it: "Everyone is entitled to his own opinion, but not his own facts." Least of all, one might add, a historian.

15. Adolf Hitler, *Mein Kampf*, excerpted in Philip Kerr, ed., *The Penguin Book of Lies* (New York: Viking, 1990), 525. Hitler contrasted the effective Allied propaganda with what he considered ineffective German propaganda. According to him, the German press depicted Allied troops as ineffective and somewhat ridiculous. When German troops confronted Allied soldiers and realized that what they had been told was untrue, they became demoralized. Elsewhere in Kerr's unusual, very useful anthology, he reprints a 1938 speech by Member of Parliament Harold Nicolson, who declared: "During the War [World War I] we lied damnably." When another member called

out, "Splendidly," Nicolson responded: "No, damnably, not splendidly," and he went on to note that a careful reading of *Mein Kampf* reveals that Hitler gained some of his ideas about propaganda and lying from the Allied effort: "[Hitler] thought it tremendous. He admired it very much" (352–354). Kerr also reprints part of the Bryce Report, the official 1915 British document containing allegations of German atrocities in Belgium and France. He notes that the report "was largely invented," particularly the repeated accusations that German troops, acting under orders, cut off civilians' hands, burned whole families alive, and bayoneted little children (294–297).

16. Gloria Steinem, *Revolution from Within* (Boston: Little, Brown, 1992), 222.

17. Naomi Wolf, *The Beauty Myth* (New York: William Morrow, 1991), 180–182 and 207 (emphasis added; obviously, Wolf intended to place blame on men, or at least to incite anger with men).

18. Joan Brumberg, *Fasting Girls: The Emergence of Anorexia Nervosa as a Modern Disease* (Cambridge: Harvard University Press, 1988), 19–20; cited in Christina Hoff Sommers, *Who Stole Feminism?* (New York: Simon & Schuster, 1994), 11.

19. For a discussion of the untruths spread about the anorexia nervosa fatalities, see Sommers, *Who Stole Feminism?*, 11–12.

20. As Ms. Kandel explained to me, this averages out to one death from an eating disorder every sixty-two minutes.

21. When her book was subsequently released in paperback, Brumberg deleted the incorrect figures about deaths from anorexia nervosa. As far as I can ascertain, however, she neither acknowledged the erroneous misinformation that had appeared in the book's hardcover edition nor explained how she came to write that 150,000 American women die annually from anorexia nervosa.

Chapter 12: Not Everything That Is Thought Should Be Said

1. Avigdor Miller, *Rejoice O Youth* (New York: 1961), 279.

2. Yitz Greenberg, "Cloud of Smoke, Pillar of Fire: Judaism, Christianity, and Modernity after the Holocaust," in *Auschwitz: Beginning of a New Era*, ed. Eva Fleischner (New York: KTAV Publishing, 1977), 25.

Chapter 13: Words That Heal—and the Single Most Important Thing to Know About Them

1. *Ethics of the Fathers* 6:3.

2. Jerusalem Talmud, *Bava Mezia* 2:11.

3. Babylonian Talmud, *Berachot* 58a.

4. *How Good Do We Have to Be?* (Boston: Little Brown, 1996) 79–80.

5. Rabbi Jonathan Sacks, "The Power of Praise," *Algemeiner*, April 20, 2018, A10.

6. Rachel Naomi Remen, *My Grandfather's Blessings* (New York: Riverhead Books, 2001), 22–24.

7. Remen, *My Grandfather's Blessings*, 22–24 (emphasis added).

8. Alan Dershowitz, *Letters to a Young Lawyer* (New York: Basic Books, 2005), 74–75 (emphasis added).

9. Stephen Carter, *Civility* (New York: Harper Perennial, 1999), 60, 62, 75.

10. Benji Levene, retold by Rabbi Jack Riemer in Jack Canfield, Mark Victor Hansen, and Rabbi Dov Peretz Elkins, *Chicken Soup for the Jewish Soul* (Deerfield Beach, FL: Health Communications, 2001), 91–94.

11. Rabbi Hanoch Teller, *And from Jerusalem His Word* (New York: New York City Publishing, 1990), 120–122.

12. Tannen, *You Just Don't Understand*, 113–114.

13. Richard E. Lapchick, "Dad," in *Sons on Fathers: A Book of Men's Writing*, ed. Ralph Keyes (New York: HarperCollins, 1992), 32–33.

14. Allen Sherman, "A Gift of Laughter," in *Growing Up Jewish: An Anthology*, ed. Jay David (New York: William Morrow, 1996), 63–66.

15. Rabbi Lawrence Kushner, *Invisible Lines of Connection* (Woodstock, VT: Jewish Lights, 1998), 81.

16. Aaron Lazare, *On Apology* (New York: Oxford University Press, 2004), 187–188.

17. When you have hurt someone in public, the apology should be offered in public. Lord Beaverbrook, the renowned British newspaper publisher, happened to meet Edward Heath—later the British prime minister but then a young member of Parliament—in a washroom of his London club a few days after Beaverbrook had published a rather insulting editorial about Heath. Embarrassed by the tone of his editorial, Beaverbrook said to Heath, "My dear chap, I've been thinking it over, and I was wrong. Here and now, I wish to apologize." "Very well," said Heath. "But next time, I wish you'd insult me in the washroom, and apologize in your newspaper." Clifton Fadiman, *Bartlett's Book of Anecdotes* (Boston: Little, Brown, 1985), 47.

18. Lazare, *On Apology*, 142.

19. David G. Dalin and Alfred J. Kolatch, *The Presidents of the United States and the Jews* (Middle Village, NY: Jonathan David Publishers, 2000), 136.

20. Where you can't undo the damage—perhaps you spread a rumor that destroyed someone's reputation, or you drove irresponsibly and hit a pedestrian or another driver, paralyzing them—apologize and do whatever you can. Unfortunately, sometimes there is not much you can do—hence the need to be careful *before* you say or do something that would inflict irrevocable damage.

   If you have destroyed another's reputation, one thing you can do is to make known to as many people as possible that what you said or did was wrong. This conclusion seems so obvious that I can hardly imagine anyone opposing it, but it has in fact been opposed by the American Civil Liberties

Union in the case of Elizabeth Richardson of Lexington, Nebraska, who was convicted of having brought a false charge of rape against Gary Nitsch. The judge ordered Richardson to pay to publish four newspaper advertisements in the local county newspapers admitting what she had done and clearing the defamed man's name. The ACLU, well aware that Nitsch had lost his job as a result of the accusations and that his children were harassed at school, insisted that the judge had no right to order any such action by the woman. Fortunately, the ACLU did not prevail, and Ms. Richardson (who filed the false charge in hopes that she would get more attention from her husband) did run the ads apologizing for her false charges against Nitsch. See Alan Dershowitz's discussion of this case in *Contrary to Popular Opinion* (New York: Pharos Books, 1992), 296–298.

21. The first half of this section is based on a video I did for Prager University entitled "What Did Your Parents Most Want You to Be?," available on YouTube at https://www.youtube.com/watch?v=5adJxEWLFKU. I want to thank Dennis Prager and Allen Estrin of Prager University for their editing and production of this video.

22. Phil Arvia, "A Proud Father," in *Chicken Soup for the Baseball Fan's Soul*, ed. Jack Canfield et al. (Cos Cob, CT: Blacklist, 2012), 71–75.

23. Cantor Malovany participated in a videotape discussing the advice offered him by the Rebbe and how it impacted and, in some ways, transformed his relationship with his son. See "Super-Connected," December 10, 1989, at https:chabad.org/1744438.

24. This section on the use of positive language is based on chapter 7, "Optimism and the Careful Choosing of Words," in my earlier book, *Rebbe: The Life and Teachings of Menachem M. Schneerson, the Most Influential Rabbi in Modern History* (New York: Harper Wave, 2014), 109–117.

25. Rabbi Abraham J. Twerski, M.D., *Do Unto Others: How Good Deeds Can Change Your Life* (Kansas City: Andrews McMeel Publishing, 1997), 3–5.

Chapter 14: Incorporating the Principles of Ethical Speech into Daily Life

1. Apocrypha, *Ecclesiasticus* 19:10.
2. Solomon Schimmel, *The Seven Deadly Sins* (New York: Free Press, 1992), 83.
3. Harold Kushner, *When All You've Ever Wanted Isn't Enough* (New York: Pocket Books, 1987), 187.

Index